My Journey Into Ashtanga Yoga

By

Kino MacGregor

Harmony Publishing
United Kingdom

Harmony Publishing,
25 Rodney Street,
Edinburgh,
EH7 4EL
Scotland,
UK.

Sacred Fire - My Journey Into Ashtanga Yoga
By Kino MacGregor

ISBN 978-1-906828-04-2

You can purchase Kino's products online at:

USA / Canada
www.kinoyoga.com

UK / Europe
www.theyogashop.co.uk

To my teacher Sri K. Pattabhi Jois who lived his
life of selfless service in the name of Ashtanga Yoga and gave
me the honor of sharing this tradition, and my teacher
R.Sharath Jois, for believing in me before
I believed in myself.

To my parents, John and Kino MacGregor, who have
loved me every day of my life.

To my husband, Tim Feldmann, who has been with me every
step of the way and who fills my life with love and joy.

"If we practice the science of yoga, which is useful to the entire human community and which yields happiness both here and hereafter - if we practice it without fail, we will then attain physical, mental, and spiritual happiness, and our minds will flood towards the Self."

—Sri K. Pattabhi Jois

"This tissue of the body is a limited expression of the divine potential, which must recover its super conscious awareness; and my asana is a practice of making it aware, my mind dwelling on it helps to infuse that awareness, and as I stretch it I consecrate the very substance of my body to the divine presence. I feel the divine presence in my heart with love, I offer my body and its stretch and its sensation in that love and my mind dwells in the sense of oneness. It is a meditation, a profound meditation including the body, the emotions and the mind –my whole being one pointed in union dwelling on the One."

—Sri Sraddhalu Ranade, December 2008, Lonavla, India

"There is a vitality, a life force that is translated through you into action. And because there is only one of you in all time, this expression is unique, and if you block it, it will never exist through any other medium and be lost."

—Martha Graham

CONTENT

INTRODUCTION

The Eastern fascination with the lotus flower comes not only from the beauty of the species, but from the sum of the flower's evolution. In the muddy, diseased waters of swamps and back rivulets all across Asia, one flower emerges unscathed from its dank origins. If you traverse the paths of undeveloped dirt roads in towns that progress left behind, the last thing you could imagine is the beauty of a flower. Yet in the same waters where petrochemicals divulge the waste of capitalist colonization and fecal matter merges with a riverbed, a sturdy seed sprouts an impossible stalk. Through the weighty, murky flotilla of insects, frogs, fish, mud, plastic, bacteria, bodies and stench there arises a clean mast of unmistakable grandeur—the lotus flower. It isn't the number of petals, nor their color or aroma, that has designed the lotus as a spiritual symbol. Instead, it is the impossibility of the blossom's beatific rise out of such muddy, soiled foundation that begets its timeless admiration. The peaceful juxtaposition of the flower's poised, reticent grace against the putrid, turgid steaming mass of muck below makes the picture so revealing and endearing to the human condition. The lotus flower is dependent, really, on only one thing to show its beauty—light. Sunlight to be exact. It will wait all day to open its bloom and hide through the night in a silent, secretive pod until the perfect mix of warmth opens the grace within. While I lived in a city full of light and endless summer sunshine, I had to travel all the way to India to find a sun warm enough to seduce my inner lotus into full bloom.

* * *

In May 2009 sixty people sat in somber silence on the honey colored bamboo floors of Miami Life Center, the yoga center on Miami Beach my husband and I created in honor of my yoga teacher Sri K. Pattabhi Jois. We gathered on the day of his death to pay our respects to the man whose unwavering dedication to yoga changed each of our lives. Images of ten trips to India flooded my mind with hues of teal blue, fluorescent orange and henna red. So many memories marked the end of an era. The chaos of the country mixed with yoga's power of transformation and my teacher's often prophetic words of wisdom coloured the future with the same inspiration that shaped me in the past. His name, Guruji to me and so many others, rang in my soul like a timeless call to grace, power, peace and beauty.

I heard his words when I was at a loss for them myself. "Yoga is possible for anybody who really wants it. Yoga is universal. Yoga is not mine," Sri K. Pattabhi Jois often said. Now more than ever the truth of Jois's statement was evident. As a lifelong student of Jois, the essence of Ashtanga yoga—the style of yoga to which he devoted his life—now rests firmly in my heart just as it does for every dedicated student and teacher of this lineage. Jois taught Ashtanga yoga for more than seventy years before passing on May 18, 2009. I traveled to Mysore, India for the first time at the age of twenty-two to study with Jois. Young, innocent and totally naive, I asked Guruji for guidance, and in him I found a true teacher. It was my great fortune to consider this amazing man my teacher from such an early age and I attribute the depth of my personal practice and teaching to the light that Guruji's fire ignited within me. Without Guruji I doubt if I would be doing yoga today.

I journeyed to Mysore, India, one last time in my teacher's honor for a memorial service. Jois's legendary life was celebrated with hundreds of Ashtangis joining the Jois family and a dozen Brahmin priests for Vaikunta Samaradhane. When I arrived with my husband, Tim Feldmann and my friend and colleague Greg Nardi we were greeted by the full spectrum of Ashtanga yoga practitioners from around the world. The multinational conglomeration of young and old faces converged on this small town in Southern India for one purpose—to honor the teacher who had been their trusted guide in yoga and life.

A catalyst for the healing process of yoga, Guruji lead me to know myself deeply and confront the inner world that I had been running from for my entire life. Through yoga I watched my body change from a foreign entity that I feared and was ashamed of to a friend I count on every day and enjoy spending time with. Yoga led me from abusive relationships to happy ones.

When I first started practicing yoga I had no idea that I entered an age-old tradition, but I quickly found out that Ashtanga yoga traces its lineage to an ancient sage named Vamana Rishi. It was in New York City where I learned that Ashtanga Yoga is a style of yoga that comes from a direct lineage of teachers, of which the living master is Sri K. Pattabhi Jois who lives in a small city called Mysore in South India. His teacher was a man called Krishnamacharya who is known as the source of most of the yoga that is now popularly taught in the West. His students have formed Iyengar yoga, Viniyoga and Ashtanga yoga. Krishnamacharya's teacher was Rama Mohana Brahmachari who lived in a cave in the Himalayas. Lineage in yoga is much like tracing a family tree. You learn from a teacher who is a student of one master. The master who is your teacher's teacher was once a student of a master as well. So it goes in an unbroken line from teacher to student back nearly 5,000 years through Indian history. Preserved without the ease of computers, typeface printing machines and backup space on external hard disks, most yoga knowledge comes from the teacher enforcing memorization on their students. I memorized the order of the postures, the breathing techniques, the focal points, the chants, the stories and anything else my teacher wanted me to. And I smiled because I was part of something timeless, meaningful and direct.

Ashtanga literally means eight limbs and is defined by the sacred yogic text, Patanjali's Yoga Sutras as Yama (moral codes), Niyama (self-purification and study), Asana (posture), Pranayama (breath control), Pratyahara (sense control), Dharana (concentration), Dhyana (meditation) and Samadhi (total peace). Ideally teachers are well versed in all eight limbs before they begin teaching so that they may truly guide the student through the entire journey of yoga.

Ashtanga yoga is broken up into six segments of postures. The first group of postures is called the Primary Series and is a pretty strenuous exercise routine. Most people will spend their entire lives working on elements of this set of seventy-two postures. Ashtanga yoga asks you to work on the spiritual through the physical. You begin by sweating your way through some yoga postures while concentrating your mind on your body, breathe and gaze. The

Primary Series of Ashtanga Yoga contains all the necessary elements for establishing health and purifying your body. It includes forward bending, twisting, backwards bending, lifting, headstanding, and the Sun Salutation or Surya Namaskara.

Since the time I first started practicing yoga the prevalence of knowledge, teachers, students, products and information about yoga has increased tenfold. My story chronicles the nearly eight-year sojourn through the peaks and valleys of the soul that has been my focus over the last portion of my life. And, as in any good story, we must start at the very beginning.

CHAPTER ONE
EVERYBODY STARTS SOMEWHERE

The neon lights across the causeway to Miami Beach shine purple– to this day an emblem of the city's magical power of attraction. With so much skin on so little solid ground, the Floridians that call this place home certainly know how to be free. Countless topless bodies fill the nearly 200-city block length of beaches and overflow onto sidewalks, cafes and shops. Eating outdoors in the hottest days of summer tempts even the most reserved to undress. Clothing once deemed necessary to preserve dignity, suddenly sheds, falling to the ground with the weight of sea-salty sweat. A bikini top is usually fine for lunch. Starting in June, the thick summer air descends on the small sandy island, chasing away the New York snow birds who have infested the beaches for the winter season. Only the local varieties remain.

Wherever water, beaches and naked bodies mesh chances are there is a good party town. From southern Europe's infamous Ibiza to Bali's international rave and surf scene to India's Portuguese hybrid hippie zone Goa, an easy hit for the night crawling rompers awaits. Miami's South Beach is certainly not the exception to this rule–more the standard. At any hour of any day of the week you can be sure of one thing in Miami, namely, that there's a house music party happening somewhere with a pretty good groove going on. It is in the deep thumping rhythm of these dance floors and palm trees that I start my journey.

The June air in Miami is saddled with the thick, voluptuous smell of night blooming jasmine almost to the point of obscenity. The sweat collects in the center of every woman's chest, sparkling like a diamond under the colorful neon lights. As air-conditioned coolness encloses life behind doors, a new appreciation for slowness unfolds in each step. The languid nature of life in the tropics is unavoidable. Close the door quickly, get in or get out.

I am twenty-two years old and I am about to walk into my first yoga class. It took me three months of walking by a sign that read "Guided

Ashtanga yoga with Ryan Tuesday/Thursday 6:30 PM" before I could get it together and walk in. The sign happens to be on a street that is on my daily route, and given that the building is a historic Spanish villa (a style I tend to admire) I seem repeatedly lured there. I turn down a side entrance, behind a few storefronts and pass a broken fountain with standing water and mosquitoes. Hiding shiny, stretchy red gym shorts and a small black sports-bra under a white tank top, I enter a realm removed from the street outside. Double wooden doors about twenty years old, recently repainted white, lead me into a waiting room, a check-in desk and various yoga-related knick-knacks. Virtually ignorant of yoga though quite opinionated, I have mixed feeling about the photos of strange men in the accouterments of holiness. Leftover hippies in loin clothes stretch into postures of unimaginable dexterity along with fat men and beards with a soft gaze in the eye. Statues of elephants standing on one leg, dancing to a silent beat, sit next to a vase with three-day-old Gerber daisies sweltering in the moisture-laden room. The floors are wood veneer, a cheap cover for the concrete below. The yellow orange walls that mimic sunshine (or spiritual light) and are dare enough to mask the stains from feet.

I pay for one class and a rental mat. I am just trying this out. Although I wasn't raised with any religion I always considered myself a spiritual person. Yet something seems fishy about entering a space created, preserved and practiced by the Hindus on the other side of the world. I imagine myself as open-minded as any person with freewill and no connection to a church or synagogue. And yet, more poignant than the fear of entering a new religion, or even considering its relevance (like many who attend their first yoga class) I am absolutely terrified of looking like a fool. Already everyone else seems to know what is going on. Most people are older, wear more placid color schemes and show less skin. They withdraw their sheathe-like mats from stealthy carrying cases. I have the odd smelling loaner mat. They sit with their legs folded under, with eyes closed, apparently in some blissful state. In this dimly lit saint-infested room a bunch of Westerners seem to be praying to some deity I have never met nor heard of. And I just want to do is yoga—you know, the bending and stretching part—whatever that entails.

The mats are arranged in long rows facing each other. The walls are already glistening with the sweaty remnants of the previous yogis' exertions. I take a spot towards the front of the room, close to a table with flowers, statues and photos of strange people with dark skin. I wait for the teacher while standing up, nervous, not wanting to look dumb, utterly self-conscious.

A man with a classical aquiline nose enters the room. His skin is evenly tanned a tawny brown and littered with star clusters of freckles. The black brown hair falls in rivulets around his chin, gracing his shoulders. He looks at ease. His eyes are infinitely black, his limbs move with grace and his presence envelopes the room, covering the students, the floors, the photos, even the dying flowers. He walks up to me and offers a casual smile.

"Have you ever done yoga before?"

"No," I manage, "not really."

"Hmmm," he says beaming, "well, do what you can."

And he is off to the front.

In the openness I mildly panic. What have I gotten myself into that I cannot get out of? I almost leave right then and there, and yet, the symbolic value of yoga is in my consciousness on some level, even then. I had, in the past, tried the meditations, the postures and other techniques at home on my own. But my interest was brief. Now I find myself like so many others, leaning on yoga in a crunch—desperate for answers, serenity, completeness. I am standing on my mat waiting, wondering which divinity will walk in, take over and save me. I once heard a rumor about an elephant god named Ganesh, who allegedly removes obstacles along one's path. An elephant is just about the scariest thing I can imagine facing right now. Besides, I doubt it would fit through the doors unless it smashed the walls down. And what about the Buddha? If he appeared would he turn all my confusion into clarity? I take a deep breath, trying to calm my nerves. I feel no spiritual presence, no Ganesh or Buddha. There is just me, my breath, my body, my mind—and the beginning of a very long journey to the center of my soul.

I begin moving. My focus shifts out of the teacher, the other students and the shabby room into an internal domain. I breathe, jump, twist, bend, fall, explore, and gaze for two hours. Two profoundly sweaty hours. At the end of class I sit like a wet dog perched on my loaner mat in disgrace. This, I tell myself, is yoga, and I feel something special, unique, and powerfully engaging about it. Later I discover that I have attended an advanced Ashtanga Yoga Primary Series class, which is a little like going straight into the Petite Elegro and Grand Jet-Jumping without any training in classical ballet. But I love a challenge and am instantly hooked.

* * *

One of the first things you should know about me is that I always had issues with my body, and I was always struggling with diet and exercise. I am, or was, like so many women, insecure about body image. On the day that I walked into my first yoga class my body was tired. I had digested a full course of fitness crazes where the span and diversity would give even a person with a strong stomach a case of indigestion. From jazzercise to spinning, the stair-master to zumba nation, kick boxing to curves, Pilates to budokon and of course lastly—to yoga—I tried it all. There always seemed to be a newer, trendier way to kick my lazy butt into shape and help me feel the burn. I, being a young woman on Miami Beach, was a particularly tantalizing target for the endless advertisements that promised a soft, supple body in a state of toned hardness.

While in this capacity I once considered myself a bit obsessed, I know that I am not alone here. Most women at some point of another have dieted, exercised, starved themselves, hated their bodies, altered their appearance and done everything within their power to beat their body into submission to an external standard of beauty, or at least into a smaller size.

From an early age I truly believed that I had fat in all the wrong places. The size and shape of my body was often occupying a major portion of my spare time. I remember a pivotal shift of consciousness occurred when, at eleven years old, a family friend said she thought I was "getting a little chubby" and should try to exercise more. While those words were spoken casually and probably (hopefully) meant to inspire a positive attitude towards health and fitness, this well-intended comment ignited a war with my body that I am still healing from today. Not only was I obsessed with physical beauty as a teenager, but I was also very aware of the many ways in which I did not feel beautiful myself.

After the Category five Hurricane Andrew knocked out electricity in Miami for nearly a month, my Dad asked me if I wanted to go to the gym with him. Having little else to do after school, I tagged along and got used to the feeling of it. Then, when I was seventeen, I got accepted at Wesleyan, a small school in Connecticut. While I was excited to wander off to New England to study, upon arrival I felt cold, alone and oddly out of place. The majority of students came from wealthy prep schools in the Northeast and I felt like just another tanned girl from Florida. As such, I found a home in two things: my studies and the gym. With a newfound zeal, only a few friends and little else to do in the snow, I threw myself into a rigor that trained my mind and worked my body. In some ways I carved out the strange combination that would later define my life in yoga.

A year later, sick of the cold, I transferred to The University of Miami, moved out on my own and continued my practiced pattern. I exercised regularly and studied hard. But it was not with the healthiest state of mind. Instead every calorie burned was a victory against my body and further ingrained a sense of self-hatred. Of course, I now understand that while focusing on calories does set a measurable goal, it also places your sole attention on burning energy and transforms exercise into a fitness enterprise that sometimes disregards health and happiness along the way. In a short time, I learned to think of my body in terms of numbers, digits and measurements, and in doing so, I missed out on a far deeper relationship, one that recognizes the body as a spiritual home in the physical world. Exercise can be much more than simply a way to burn calories and whip oneself into shape. It can evolve into a way of making peace with yourself, your body and your world in a very deep way. But it took me many years of yoga practice to really figure all that out.

During college, exercise used to be a kind of penance I accepted for the crime of imagined plumpness. The world where I used to live had a paradigm of self-denigration that used exercise as a punishment for not being perfect and worthy. I always thought I would finally be happy and peaceful one day when I burned off enough fat. I never imagined that it was possible to be happy with the body that I had. I worked myself hard every day in an attempt to force my body into a form that I was happy with, hoping that happiness in a broader sense would come with that "perfect" form.

What was missing from my exercise routine was an appreciation of the beauty that I do have, of the body that is mine and the person that I was and am. There is no amount of sweat-induced calorie burning that can possibly reshape our soul. And yet when I first experienced Sukhasana, known as the final relaxation that comes at the end of every Ashtanga yoga class, I felt such a deep sense of unity. In a world illuminated by artificial lighting, the subtle soft and inviting darkness of this moment of rest instilled a sense of health and healing. These five to ten minutes shrouded in silence gave my body its first taste of regeneration, my mind the space to rest and my soul a home to embody. With my eyes closed after this two-hour sweating I was filled with a strikingly new clarity. I felt more comfortable in my body than I ever had before. And then the teacher led us in the final closing with the traditional salutation of all yoga practice, which is "Namaste" and means the divine light in me salutes and honors the divine light within you.

That summer night in Miami was life altering for me. Through rain, increasing heat, tropical storms and tourist masses I began attending this class twice a week for three months. In the beginning I was the student that every yoga center dreams of. I spoke emphatically to everyone I knew about my new hobby and brought all my friends to class. Like an immature convert I grew more fanatical than the fundamentalists and could not believe it when someone told me that they'd never tried yoga before. The truth was that I felt so great that I just wanted to share yoga with everyone. With a genuine beginner's enthusiasm, I reached out into the world with all the infantile knowledge of a novice and shared whatever I possibly could.

In the beginning I bought yoga mats, yoga books, yoga posters and yoga DVDs with little or no discriminating wisdom but like any novice I found my path. I slowly began to see that yoga asks that you develop a real, intimate relationship with yourself, first and foremost. The daily discipline of a committed practice over a long period of time allows practitioners to get to know themselves on a day-today basis. You see, I have come to learn that yoga uses the bodily exercises as a means to an end. In a sense, the physical side of yoga is a road to the spiritual, not a separate entity but an intricately connected experience that comes with each breathe and posture. When I practice yoga now, I literally knock at the door of new possibilities every day. A new way of movement requires me to learn new ways of thinking, feeling and being with my body. As such, every new posture literally rearranges the mind, body connection in which the human spirit lives. By using the physical postures not as ends, in and of themselves, but as tools to teach the skills needed to live a peaceful life in tune with your deepest sense of self, yoga itself becomes the catalyst for self-realization.

While I spent years devoted to other forms of fitness it was not until I found yoga that I was able to develop a healthy sense of self and make peace with my body. For example, one of the main principles I find missing from most contemporary approaches to exercise is the creation of a stable sense of self built from the inside out. If you start an exercise routine without a sense of self love, that your body isn't acceptable as is, then the stage is set for failure. You see, the body and mind are connected at a very deep level. How you feel, think and act help determine your posture, health and fitness. It's simply not enough to plug away mindlessly at fitness routines without addressing the deeper aspect of your thoughts, about your reasons for your daily disciplines. When I began to embrace this kind of thinking my yoga practice transformed my life in subtle, yet powerful ways. While the actual practice only took up an hour and a half of my life, the effect lasted much longer. Since yoga actually trains the mind to think, be and act in a different way during each breath, one yoga practice in the morning can set the practitioner up for handling their day quite differently than what they initially had in mind. Yoga literally teaches how to act, be and react in new ways.

Contemporary notions of exercise often have an external standard of beauty as their stated goal rather than health. Yet a perfect physical form simply cannot be attained. Nature has variety and imperfection. Ashtanga yoga challenges the notion of what physical perfection really means. With a daily practice Ashtanga practitioners are faced with their imperfections and forced to make peace with what they can and cannot accomplish while quietly and persistently asking their bodies to perform more complex postures. When I attempted Ashtanga yoga there was so much that I thought would always be impossible and through the process of attempting these seemingly impossible feats I learned how to make peace with myself.

Yoga taught me to see the perfection in imperfection, and embrace my body as it was. And, one of the amazing results I came to see was that the very instant I totally accepted my body for what it was, it changed to be stronger, leaner and more flexible. It truly did. But it was not until I had entirely surrendered to the self that I was, that change actually occurred. Five years after I started practicing yoga I remember a moment when I looked in the mirror and felt, perhaps for the first time in my life, really beautiful. This was such a shock that I almost didn't recognize the person that was smiling back at me. I really truly was, a different person, and the change had allowed the beauty that I carried within me throughout my whole life to finally shine through.

CHAPTER TWO
YOGA IN THE BIG APPLE

The same year I stretched and sweat in Ryan's "Guided Ashtanga" class I traveled north, abandoning the neon of Miami for the everything of New York City. Like any newcomer I spent my first two weeks taking pictures of everything. Yellow, white and pink flowers in massive planters contrasted sharply with the silver and grey glimmering buildings behind them. I immediately found myself overwhelmed by the pace of the average New Yorker; a pace that had little time for getting lost in the urban maze of Manhattan.

The purpose of my move was to get a graduate degree at NYU in Interdisciplinary Studies but as I sought to "find myself" through my studies and internships in the "big apple", what found me was more yoga. It didn't take long before I joined the mat-carrying members of the yoga scene in lower Manhattan. Like everything else in New York, yoga was fast, intensive, filled with innuendo, attitude, learning, enthusiasm, possibility and raw potential. For all the yoga classes South Beach advertised, New York offered more styles, more methods, and with that came more classmates, competition and less space to stretch my body. This was a city that had everything, available whenever I needed it, but with that came eight and half million people—and it turned out a lot of them also liked yoga. It didn't take long for me to realize that New York had a steady pulse, and you could feel its energy vibrating along every street and around every corner.

The first yoga class I attended in New York felt like coming home. The doors of an old elevator creaked open revealing a landing with a copper colored obelisk desk. The sound of falling water filled the room. An enormous, wall size waterfall cascaded behind the desk, over metal statues of Ganesh and Shiva. I fell in love instantly. Although I had only the pop-culture notion of these Hindu deities I felt like it was me that was being baptized repeatedly in their presence. I was so new to the cacophony of New York's honking taxis and moaning city buses, weaving cyclists and disgruntled pedestrians. Hip-hop tunes pulsed from car stereos that merged at traffic lights, passing the swift melodies of salsa blaing from corner bodegas. I found it overwhelming. In all of it, I was desperate for a morsel of serenity. Beyond the gushing waterfall at Jivamukti Yoga Center, the pace and the pushiness of Manhattan seemed to fade away entirely. It was here, I like to think, that I finally began to hear the voice of my own inner guidance.

I should mention that the center that I joined was not the average hole-in-the-wall, run down yoga studio that I was used to. Located in Union Square, Jivamukti Yoga Center was New York's finest merger of yoga and business—East meets West. Immediately evident to me was absence of preconceived notions that I had attached to the spiritual side of yoga. Instead I found people who were searching and lost, just like me, finding themselves through their devotion to yoga. For the first time in my life I experienced a sense of authentic kinship. It was within the walls of this yoga community that I found the support, guidance and friendship that aided me on my path of inner discovery.

I will never forget the day when I decided to attend the early morning Ashtanga Yoga class called "Mysore Style." This particular yoga is the most traditional and intensive form of Ashtanga, and requires that you not only commit yourself to various bending, twisting and lifting positions but that you also memorize the list of postures you try to contort yourself into six days a week. Mysore Style Ashtanga Yoga asks for near contortionist flexibility while you face your own weakness and stiffness. It is not every yoga practitioner who finds a home in the midst of such feverish dedication, but my competitive nature did and I continue to devote myself to it today. When I first arrived for the Mysore Style class with my small cheat sheet that I studied on the subway ride over an odd combination of excitement and dread flooded through me. As my hand touched the door handle, my heart skipped a beat and my breath retracted into a knot at the back of my throat. Exhaling, I turned the handle and entered the already sweaty room. Stretched out in front of me on yoga mats set distances apart, nearly fifty people were deep into their twists and turns already. A woman was bent inside out with both legs behind her head and a man balanced on his hands in a perfect handstand. They looked like circus performers to me and I couldn't imagine ever achieving anything close to such feats. For a moment I wondered if I had come to the right class but quickly dismissed that notion and claimed an empty space on the hardwood floor. My hands shook as I unrolled my mat.

Class was a blur. I remember we practiced almost entirely in silence. While my body moved and my mind focused, my spirit—this mysterious other part of me—a part that up until that moment I hadn't really considered, seemed to awaken. It's hard to explain, really, except to say that I immediately felt that a long neglected portion of who I was had at last been recognized. I knew I would be back the next day. There was an atmosphere of authenticity to the class that seduced me, and Mysore Yoga became my new spiritual addiction.

At the end of class, a small, relatively young man stood at the edge of my mat and spoke with uncompromising authority.

"This class meets six days a week; you can come at 8 AM".

Characteristically Japanese, Govinda Kai, spoke slowly and maintained a samurai's unreadable smile. He moved with a grace mirrored by the soundless space of the class. Dark hair in an Aikido master's ponytail, stone-faced with almost unnoticeable upturned smiling lips, a communicative touch and a wisdom exuding real world experience, Govinda let the attraction of the class speak for itself. He did not wait for my reply to his invitation but simply walked away with the full confidence that I would return the next day. And of course I did. I also never forgot Govinda, and to this day think of him as an incredible teacher who truly changed my life.

In his class I felt like I had joined the Cirque du Soleil. Each time I showed up for class the raw power of the group was palpable. The grace and fluidity of the flowing practice performed in silence moved the Earth under my feet. Mysore Style Ashtanga yoga asks that each individual work in silence so that students can truly focus inward. The theory is that, in doing so, students have the experience of being on their own in a group setting. This sense of isolation allows practitioners to feel their own bodies and direct their minds to the internal workings of their souls. With the help of a qualified teacher students can go, or meditate, much more deeply into their bodies, progress even faster along the set series of postures that is Ashtanga yoga and feel even more peace of mind. It's worth mentioning that Mysore Style Ashtanga yoga is based on the notion of repeating the same series of postures. The idea is that eventually the student is no longer listening to the teacher for instruction on what to do next because he or she has the order of postures memorized; therefore, the body and mind are able to elevate to a new level of consciousness. The mind is directed inward and the body flows through a familiar series of movements. In the simplest of terms—the emphasis is on meditation. There is no music, no distraction, just you, your breath and your body.

Four more days of Mysore Style Ashtanga Yoga practice and I was so sore that I could barely lift a glass of water or put on mascara without resting my elbow on the sink ledge. Walking down or up stairs without my legs quivering from pain was impossible. Yet as I continued through my first week of what amounted to yoga boot camp I learned what is perhaps the first lesson of yoga, that is, to accept the pain that arrives as part of your learning process. While you never have to invite pain into your experience (it arrives all on its own without any beckoning), when it does arrive let it teach you and make you stronger. Pain broke me down to a point where I was willing to ask for help, but it would take a little longer than four days.

What turned out to be equally challenging for me was understanding the connection between the physical practice and the spiritual transformation. I have since come to respect it as one of the most mystical experiences of yoga. No one can define exactly how the body, mind and soul unite to produce enlightenment, yet practitioners all around the world experience just that. The high level of difficulty in Ashtanga Yoga combined with the fast paced order of the postures has the ability to quiet the mind dramatically. And with this newfound harmony comes an inevitable desire to carry it outside into the world beyond the classroom. But this task is easier said than done. One of the things I immediately felt when I began a daily practice of Ashtanga Yoga is how many levels there are to the body. Twisting and bending in some of the postures of the Primary Series feels like running the spot-scrubber cycle of the washing machine on your insides. And believe me it felt just like that! There is a posture called Marichyasana D that demands a deep folding and twisting into a pretzel-like position. You are then asked to relax, strengthen and remain calm for five breaths. Doing this every day made me more conscious of what might make these postures easier or harder. I found that if I got a good night's sleep life was easier on my yoga mat. If I didn't rush to the yoga center and arrived in a happy state of mind the practice flowed much more smoothly. On the other hand, if I ate two packets of Mentos in place of lunch the day before I found that this pose, Marichyasana D, was no longer my friend. Sometimes it felt like the sticky bits of all the candy I ate had congealed and formed a rebel mutant army in my innards and all I could do was twist, bend, breathe and sweat it out in an effort to make peace with the processed sugar I dared let pass my lips. I soon learned that there is no greater motivation to put the jelly beans away than to feel the obstruction they form the next day when you are doing your best to maintain a peaceful state of mind whilst pushing your absolute physical limits. In fact, it was the simple act of eating that began to lead the way towards my own spiritual transformation.

* * *

Finding the ability to meditate, to truly look inside myself, was probably the greatest lesson I took from my early months in Mysore Yoga. The spiritual side of yoga doesn't come easily and often the yogi doesn't know what they should be looking for in the first place. Sometimes it's obvious—grief over a loss or stress over a job, or addiction to drugs or alcohol. Often, however, it's not so clear when the student peers inside themselves; sometimes a problem is deeply rooted; maybe its been there forever, maybe its new but the individual don't know its there. The point is that ultimately everyone has something to find and fix, and one of my broken parts was based in the very simple notion of food.

Because eating food is an act that sustains us and because we Westerners are in the midst of an obesity crisis I thought I'd devote a little time to discussing food in the hopes that will help others who have similar problems. For me, food itself wasn't exactly the culprit, it was more what eating did to me both physically and emotionally. For as long as I can remember I loved food but had a confusing relationship with it. I grew up during the eighties when the fat free craze hit America and I watched my parents jump on every fad diet to hit the major news stands. With this as my backdrop, there grew an unwillingness to accept my body as it was. I had an unhealthy relationship with food that had its roots nestled deep. What to eat, how to eat—my entire relationship with food was like a giant riddle that no one bothered to explain to me. Now I was determined to solve it.

If you think about it, choices about food on any given day are a snapshot into one's sense of self worth. I would often eat to escape feelings of insecurity, anxiety and nervousness. It is no coincidence that when I am stressed out I tend to overeat. Sometimes pleasure, boredom, habit, guilt, escape, and addiction are the emotions of food. There are moments of unconsciousness and moments of deep communion. Cravings, addictions and destructive patterns are all part of the possible roads to travel when dealing with food.

After two months of daily Mysore Style Ashtanga Yoga practice I began to have a desire to heal my relationship with food. It was a thought that entered one afternoon, uninvited, but totally welcomed and long overdue. Back at my apartment I looked at the mountains of sugar-laden candy that lined my kitchen counters as well as the wasted food I had tossed out in the trash, worrying it had too many calories in it. I felt for the first time in my life the pain of disconnection with myself and body and I wanted to heal. So I asked the one authority I had come to trust for help. My yoga teacher, Govinda Kai, directed me towards a whole food nutritionist named Gabriel Cousens who wrote a book called Conscious Eating.

Through Cousens' book I began to see that every bit of food contains the entire socioeconomic system of its creation. Within the first month of practicing daily Mysore Style Ashtanga Yoga I gave up poultry and switched to soy milk. Within six months of committed practice I said goodbye to "real" sushi and went entirely vegetarian; Cousens' book, which raises the red flag on animal cruelty, touched my heart so deeply so that I wanted nothing more than to stop harming animals by eating them. I'll never forget where he suggested that if the entire human population were vegetarian there would be no world hunger since the amount of grain it takes to feed American livestock could feed the world's hungry two times over. For the first time in my life, I became conscious of what I was eating on a macroscopi level.

While I was no novice to the diet and exercise game I was new to yoga and the nutritional framework of the yogic lifestyle. To complicate things, there are at least a dozen new diets every year promising to make you forever young, cancer-free, heart healthy, thin, vibrant and closer to God. The yoga world is not free of unbalanced dietary regimes by any stretch. In fact, it often encourages various cleansing and detoxification programs. My teacher, for example, was a raw foodist, which requires a very strict diet; the idea here is that the closer a food item is to its original source, i.e., the sun via photosynthesis, the closer it is to God. In order to be spiritually evolved the raw foodies believe that human beings should not process their foods at all—a veggie stir-fry with tofu becomes a sin.

It took me many months of experimentation, selection and deletion to find a healthy balanced diet. Even so, to this day I have to admit that fruit and nuts are probably my favorite foods and if I could live healthfully as fruitarian I would. But the ups and downs of life, the need for more protein and my powerful sweet tooth has me unwilling to make such a commitment. Ultimately food represents two things for me: trust and control. Before I started practicing yoga I simply did not trust my body enough to hand over the daily routines of life to it because I believed that if I did I would not be beautiful. It is not a happy thought to think or to carry around and I am not proud of the fact that I expended so much energy trying to make my body into something that it was not. But I did and I am sharing it here with the intention that someone may read this and find inspiration to make the major lifestyle change that need to happen for true health to take long-term residence in the body.

Yoga helped me grasp the idea that the body is simply a vehicle created to house the spirit; it receives nourishment to produce energy in the world. Once I understood this I began saying a prayer of thanks before eating. A friend then pointed out to me that by praying before my meals I was, in turn, creating an act of self-love, that self-love is eating healthfully and caring for the body. Still, my problems were not entirely solved. Like most people concerned with their weight, one of my great challenges was healing the unhealthy image I had created of myself. I began to see that all the various diets I'd tried were ultimately rejecting my basic worthiness. Therefore I was doomed for failure. I had always been the sort of person who would make radical all-or-nothing changes for a few weeks or month and then fall off the wagon and eat a chocolate muffin or five. For me, it wasn't going to be enough to simply change the food I ate or become conscious of it—no—I wasn't going to heal until I found a way to transform the thoughts I kept guarded under lock and key in my mind. I really do believe that all food choices are reflections of self-love, self-acceptance and self-appreciation. Without learning love and appreciation, no diet can create joy and lasting happiness.

This understanding brought me to the simple theory that at the core of every unhealthy relationship with food is a cluster of negative thoughts that amount to a fundamental rejection of who you really are. You just feel really bad about life. Up until I redefined food as a form of nourishment and a deep communication and communion with the world around me I thought of the epicurean in me as bad and unworthy because these cravings would make me grow horizontally at the waist. Yet what I did and could not see is that whenever you cast a part of yourself out as bad and evil there is a divisive pattern that drives your whole life askew. The very notion of dieting includes a de facto recognition of oneself as bad. In my case, even when I was at my thinnest I was still unhappy because I never addressed the voice inside my head that told me I was not good enough.

What I could not see, that yoga helped me see, is that what really matters is how you feel along the journey of life. Health and happiness are part and parcel of a total life perspective that includes genuine gratitude for the gift of life.

I talked earlier about how the dynamic power of Ashtanga Yoga demands that you be totally conscious and present in your body when you practice. If you are out of balance you feel it immediately. After a while you begin to notice just how bad a heavy late-night meal makes you feel early in the morning or the lingering effects of alcohol and drugs. Yoga asks you to honestly feel your body, its emotions and the particles moving in and out every day and every minute–air, water, food. What is taken in must also be released for the body to remain in dynamic balance. Food is just one of many ways that we exchange and communicate with the world. While few physical objects penetrate as deeply into the physical body as food does, there are thoughts, emotions and sensations that touch the soul. The act of eating is a blending and an intimacy perhaps only paralleled by sex. If you were to think about eating habits and food consumption as a sacred act of intimacy expressed between two lovers, certainly the act of eating takes on a whole new perspective.

But yoga itself is no magic solution. Yoga paves the way for life transformations only if students are willing to apply the lessons learned on the mat to every experience throughout the day. I had been practicing yoga for a year and a half before I began to make peace with food and to love my myself both inside and out. But this didn't happen in a day, in a moment–in fact, I'm not exactly sure when the transformation occurred.

I just know I found myself back in Miami with a Master's degree from NYU and I began to see that my love/hate relationship with food was simply a conditioned behavior. It could be changed. Slowly I started to see that I was no longer the victim of circumstance but a powerful player in the game of life. I went from feeling powerless to feeling powerful. I recognized that a habit is behavioral but not essential and it is something smaller than the might and grandeur of a human being. A habit I could handle. And I did so by beginning to take responsibility for everything that crossed my lips and entered my body. What I ate I would digest, accept and integrate and thus I began the process of making peace with my food, my body and my environment.

But that pivotal moment of realization was more the culmination of a journey that would take me much further away than Miami or New York City. Before I left Manhattan I was still victim to my habits and couldn't seem to find my way in my life. The turning point for me happened when I discovered the man who was my teacher, the founder of the Ashtanga Yoga Method, Sri K. Pattabhi Jois. I heard stories of yoga students going to India to study yoga and a place inside of me yearned for that same vision quest. I wanted to become the hero of my life story. As an academic I was accustomed not just to reading, but to devouring books and spitting out quotes, information and research. With my first yoga book I wanted to read differently because I wanted to learn and integrate every morsel with my whole being. The essential book on Ashtanga Yoga, Yoga Mala, written by its master and founder Sri K. Pattahbi Jois, sat on my cheap, student bedside furniture for nearly a month before I turned the last page. I read only at night when my day was finished so that Jois' words would be the last thought on my mind before I fell asleep.

It was a rainy night late in April when I finished reading Yoga Mala. New York City had already begun its steady transformation into Spring so that the small buds of flowers perked through impossible green patches in the otherwise grey concrete world. In the yoga practice placing your hands in prayer position is also a mudra, or blessing position, known as Anjali mudra. This is said to represent the spiritual heart like a flower bud, complete with the intoxicating nectar of full fruition of the spiritual journey. My students' apartment in Battery Park gave me a rather ordinary home, supplied with university furniture. Sleeping on a particleboard twin bed with an unremarkable design surrounded by dressers, tables and chairs made out of the same forgettable wood veneer, I felt my own heart beginning to feel the awakening of a new season in my life.

On the night that I finished reading Yoga Mala, the early evening rains cleared and I stared out the window of my apartment in Battery Park; it was four months before 9/11. At first all I saw were the lights of the Trade Towers glittering in the distance. But then the moon appeared from behind the clouds and seemed to offer a soft comfort with its image. City lights converged in a flurry through the naked glass panes, sprinkling the evening with a kind of pixie dust. I placed my hands in prayer and opened my soul to the divine, hoping that my spirit would one day open and flower too.

Although it was an average city night complete with trash accumulating along the street below, take-away Chinese food wafting through the building halls and students pulling all-nighters to study for exams, I entered another world that night. I pulled the covers over my shoulders, placed Yoga Mala on my nightstand like the Bible it was becoming and surrendered my heart to the world of dreams.

Lost in the wonderland of imagination at the end of what felt like a trek across light years, I saw an image of Jois. He appeared as a redemptive figure who rescued me from the arms of an angry Shiva and placed me on a peaceful cruise ship bound for the dawn. The salvific feeling of the dream left me breathless and I awoke from this fantasy with a life-changing thought on my lips. I opened my eyes, panting, and whispered aloud, "I have to go to India."

I bought my ticket two weeks later and left three months after that for a two month trip that changed my life path forever. It was not easy to arrange a sudden trip across continents, but my choice opened doors that I did not know were there. I truly believed I was called and every step of the journey felt blessed. The decision to go to Mysore ultimately opened a doorway to my discovery of my own true power, the kind of power that knows that the human spirit is larger than any bad habit.

CHAPTER THREE
PRACTICE MAKES PERFECT

I was the shaved-head, nipple-pierced New York University graduate student in a world where nobody cared about appearances. I exited the Bangalore airport and the remnants of my feminist studies paradigm seemed to melt in the heat. After attempting sleep in various uncomfortable positions on three different airplanes, spanning thirty hours from New York City through Paris and Mumbai finally to arrive in Bangalore, I braved a midnight Indian taxi run to Mysore. An Indian driver whose grasp of the English language was more than limited led me to an old ambassador car with shag carpeting covering the seats, no AC, broken windows and a decorated pink steering wheel. This was my chariot to the city of yoga, Mysore. In less than a year I had become a devoted yogi and completed half of my Graduate degree in Interdisciplinary Studies. Now as the pre-dawn sky blushed an ethereal pink through the polluted firmament my mind acclimated to a totally undiscovered reality. A dancing elephant deity called Ganesh, remover of obstacles, jiggled and bobbled his rotund body and fat limbs; he was supposedly intended to protect us from the onslaught of vehicles, cows, goats, sheep, scooters and packs of dogs that had the potential of crashing into us on the journey. A string of yellow flowers hung as garnish on the bodice of the rearview mirror and burning incense fogged the interior of the vehicle. I wasn't totally convinced of the power of Lord Ganesh's blessing just yet.

My identification and attachment to the Western world faded with each minute and each mile. Low-striations of orange glowing clouds encased the morning solar rays. Zooming past whole villages, animal herds, tea stalls and coconut farms, the blanket of sunlight and early morning air welcomed me to a whole new way of living. Whenever I think back to that first glimpse of India I remind myself of just how unique a place it truly is. India's beauty cannot be found through the intellectual device of comparison. If you arrive there and evaluate its way, logic and tradition with the Western world, it will always fail and deliver second-rate services that drive you nuts. But if you surrender to India as it really is, that is when you will witness unspeakable grace in the grit of every corner.

Sitting there in the taxi I had to pinch myself; it was truly remarkable how the trip itself all became possible. Somehow finances were sorted out, my parents gave me their blessing and support, a sublet agreement was arranged and numerous other seemingly impossible problems were solved. I bought my airline ticket just two weeks after my fateful dream and three months later I was sitting in that taxi cab whose tires kicked up dust around every winding turn. The whole adventure was freeing, perhaps my first true taste of living an absolutely beautiful life, and the first real period in which I believed in myself.

Under a washed-out blue sky, trailing a blaze of tiredness I arrived in the small area of Mysore called Lakshmipuram where Ashtanga Yoga master Sri K. Pattabhi Jois lived and taught most of his life. Lakshmi is the Hindu deity of prosperity, beauty, abundance and money; she is shown with musical instruments, a Mona Lisa smile and golden rupees overflowing around her. I was so eager for the future that I paid the taxi and got out in front of the Ashtanga Yoga Nilayam, Sanskrit for Ashtanga Yoga Research Center. Small cream-coloured steps led up to the entrance of this building, home of yoga master Sri K. Pattabhi Jois. In typical Mysore city design the stairs to the raised front door opened outward in both directions in a gentle right and left slope, a kind of open armed hello offering a welcome embrace to visitors. Indian doors are not the harsh divisions of the West. Instead the top portion of two wooden flanks encase an extra-large netting, not small enough to keep mosquitoes out but tiny and sturdy enough to keep the monkeys, robbers and most other animals out. More a symbol of division than a real division, traditional old world Indian houses allow the outside to come inside and the inside to blur its way outside. The delineation between the two realms is soft and mellifluous, left up for your imagination, creation and use.

Voices and noises from the side of the building drew my movement forward. I took a few steps before realizing that the entrance to the yoga space was down the alley towards the left side of the building. Around an alley, down a small dirt road another pair of double doors with netting on the top half sat atop a second semi-welcoming mini-staircase. There was no grand sign announcing the residence of a yoga master; just the doors, not even a receptionist and certainly no velvet rope. Beyond these humble doors Sri K. Pattabhi Jois and his grandson and assistant Sharath Rangaswamy sat calmly and quietly. Outside I stood with my heart in my throat, speechless and eager.

In the Indian tradition of teachers and students, there is a word called "Guru" or "Guruji" which is usually attributed to higher teachers. It is also customary to put your hands on the feet of the Guru and bow. The term is used by students to their teachers as an affectionate expression describing the sacredness of the teacher student relationship. No teacher calls him or herself Guru because it is the students who make the teacher. I, being a New York feminist in the post-gender revolution world, had my qualms about all this. With my reservations in full resurrection I walked ahead despite my preconceived notions and entered the Old Shala in the Lakshmipuram neighborhood of Mysore. Jois turned and peeked out from behind an open door in the small room where twelve people were deep into the sweat of their daily yoga practice. He said, "You come to practice?"

My eyes met his and there was a recognition of the man in my yoga dreams, a being beyond gender, politics and ideas. I was already touched by the inner beauty of this man.

"Yes, you come tomorrow 8 AM," he said and as his words withdrew into the air I was on my knees, hands touching his feet, my head on the floor saying the words I used over and over throughout the next ten years of my life.

"Thank you Guruji."

* * *

The early morning air was cooled by the arrival of the monsoon season in Karnataka, the state that houses Mysore and Bangalore. Dewy, not quite chilly, dusty, smelly, thick, dense, filled with a discordant medley of sounds and the particular quality of Indian air. Passing a flock of yoga students, taxi drivers, con artists, rickshaw drivers and random on-lookers, I got the sense that the mere presence of foreigners was both an escape fantasy for the locals and a tasteless novelty.

I entered through the back staircase of the Ashtanga Yoga Nilayam and waited my turn to practice. The first yoga practice in India is like losing your virginity. It is a moment you spend hours fantasizing about and when the fateful moment comes, it is over before you know it and you are left wondering what happened, contemplating the details and replaying the event over in your head. I got a space towards the back left side of the room, next to the wall and right in front of my teacher's stool. I was dripping with nervous sweat, smiling out of excitement and terror and trembling beyond conscious control. It was time for me to join the ranks of sweaty Mysore yogis. I unrolled my mat and began the deep breathing and flowing movement that defines Ashtanga Yoga. I progressed humbly through the set series of postures that I had committed to memory until the end. The standard of Mysore meant that Guruji and his assistant Sharath would only allow students to move onto the next posture once they had attained proficiency in the preceding asanas or postures. The moments ticked by and I was not stopped as I completed the Ashtanga Yoga Primary Series. Holding my final pose I breathed a sigh of relief; it was an honor to pass the first test without being stopped for incorrectness somewhere along the way.

While I made it to the end of the first series of Ashtanga Yoga I now had to pass a more ominous test of back bending, known as Urdhva Dhanurasana. To give you a mental image, the posture is first performed from the floor with the hands and feet evenly spaced at hips width and shoulder width apart while the spine is extended or bent backwards and the body is hoisted off the ground. This heroic movement challenges even the best practitioners. But I had devoted myself to the method of Ashtanga Yoga and could already do the full bridge both from the floor and from standing up. From standing, this postures is called "drop-backs" in the Ashtanga Yoga tradition and involves standing up and dropping back from the bridge posture. At the end of the sequence the teacher then assists the student to deepen their backbend with the most advanced version of the posture being a circus-like trick where the spine is folded over itself so deeply so that the practitioner is standing on their feet with their hands holding their knees. Not an easy feat for anyone.

As I dropped from my last backbend, my hands were on the floor and my eyes drifted towards my feet. I could see my new yoga teacher's toes standing at the edge of my mat. Guruji placed his hands on my hips and said, "You go back." I went back, barely breathing, shaking to have his attention directly towards me. After three times he said, "You catch". And I released my fear in the arms of my teacher and before I could say yes or no my hands were on my knees. Peaceful in a wordless, thoughtless unity I opened my eyes and surrendered into the hug that Guruji gave his female students after deep back bending. Breathing together in an intimate space that was not defined by gender but by humanity, my heart opened even more. The tender ache inside me cracked open. He guided me to the floor for the counter stretch, forward bending, called Paschimattanasana. Laying his full weight on my back, tears that I had been holding back for lifetimes flowed freely. In his joyful spirit he said, "Good, good, best. Thank you very much."

* * *

Afterwards, I gazed around the room; the space itself was not particularly unusual. There were antique, hand-painted pictures of yogis positioned in various areas and the floors were covered with worn turquoise and red cotton rugs. The walls were painted yellow and red and a row of fluorescent lights hung from above. But what the Old Shala had was a nostalgic flavor that spoke to an era of India's history before electricity, to time when yogis lived in caves and the unbroken lineage of teachers and students of yoga was sacred and, to some degree, secret. That room where twelve students practiced at a time had an unmistakable authenticity, one that you could not manufacture even if you tried. Practicing there for the first time felt right. As I finished my practice and took rest in the final relaxation posture called Savasana, I noticed my trembling had been replaced by a warm hum. And while the sweat kept pouring off me, my smile shined from a deeper and more complete place within.

I stumbled out onto the streets of Mysore in a euphoric

post-yoga glow. If it were not for the presence of a group of hard-working yoga practitioners inhabiting a nearby circle of dilapidated chairs, I am sure I would have been the perfect travel victim. A man named Mitchell walked over and ordered me a "paper gungi" coconut and a straw. I learned later that "paper gungi" is local lingo for the youngest coconut that is filled with blissfully perfect liquid and the most tender flesh imaginable. I walked towards the other students, but most were a little on the taciturn side, choosing to keep their experiences of yoga to themselves while scoping out the newcomer with a minimal amount of dialogue. Many of these students had been in Mysore for months already and had seen the coming and going of various transitory students, visitors and travelers. I was too engrossed within my first fresh coconut to care. Being a Miami mall rat I had never tried coconut in anything other than dessert. My parents' version of East-meets-West cuisine was solely Japanese (my grandfather's heritage) and the Chinese that every American knows--wonton soup and fried rice. Fresh coconuts and the curries of India were something totally new to me. With eyes staring down the red straw I gazed into a milky pool of viscous liquid and sucked. My lips tasted a sweet richness. I swallowed, gazing into the open coconut I held in my hand. Drawing the juiciness into me again, I welcomed my first real taste of yoga in India.

* * *

Everyone thinks that going to India to study yoga will bring them closer to the source. It definitely did. But the experience of India itself is a great yoga teacher. It was perhaps the sheer magnitude of contrast between the suburban world of ease that I had known and the chaos of India that allowed me to grow the milestones I did. There is a marked difference between an American's understanding of personal space and an Indian's. America invented suburban sprawl to accommodate everyone's need for more than 3,000 square feet of living space. A typical Indian que involves a hectic shepherding of people bumping into each other at every point possible, nudging in a very directed but friendly fashion with close enough quarters to smell everyone's lunch on their breathe. Although the palm trees in Mysore brought nostalgic memories of Florida to mind, in the beginning I found myself an American princess planted in an Indian jungle.

In a kind of crash course dive into idiosyncratic India I plunged into the realities of life outside of the cultural norm of North America. This was perhaps the hardest yoga of all. The postures kept their place on the sticky mat, but my mind was with me every waking moment. I rose every morning to a luck-driven gamble with the local power authorities. Fumbling for candles in shadows whenever the power clicked off, the power cuts ignited my internal engine. I fumed in futility with no one really to blame and no possibility of changing the situation. Not only would fueling the flames of my anger not solve the problem of being stuck in the midst of a power cut controlled by a government officer far away, but allowing the emotional tide to engross and encapsulate me prevented me from hearing its subtle gift—the sounds of silence. Without my iPod, satellite TV, mobile phone and other of life's artificially induced sounds I heard crows, crickets, roosters, cows, dogs, cats, wind, my heartbeat, my breath, my thoughts and my feelings. Sometimes the power cuts would last all day. Every morning I surrendered to my teacher and every day I had no choice but to surrender to India.

Sitting in silence at newfound free moments throughout the day I had time to allow my mind to rest, reflect and dream. In every yoga practice there is at least one moment where the mind's mental chatter lifts and there is a hint at a clear, open state of consciousness. In Mysore these moments grew in each practice and expanded further into my day.

Without the usual stream of distractions I suddenly noticed how obsessed I was with beauty. Of all my obsessions, I was surprised to find the idea of beauty at the top of the list. And yet, as I meditated, I soon realized just how much I equated beauty with physical features, external possessions and achievement. It became apparent to me that two people could wear the same outfit and yet one would appear much more attractive than the other. Rather than finding a physical reason for the difference in appearance I began to notice that some people used material things as a band-aid to make them appear and feel better than they actually thought they were. In this way any inner feelings of incompleteness would be exacerbated. Through reflection, I began to see that in a world without things, one's identity and goals take up more space in their mind. This was certainly the case for me in Mysore. Before India, my whole being revolved around the myth of the American dream. We Americans are all collectively in a rush to unearth the next hidden secret and produce our very own million-dollar invention. This makes us brilliant innovators, forward thinking dreamers and daringly ambitious artists, and yet simultaneously, so many of us are history deprived, beauty-obsessed shopaholics haunting soulless strip malls sipping mass-produced lattes. It is no wonder that I had to run away to India to learn to make peace with myself. I was bitten by the consumer culture virus, the ubiquitous stream of television, music, radio and internet that engaged me, as the target demographic, to digest its whole paradigm of thought. Behind every TV show is a kind of think tank targeting often unspoken cultural assumptions and ideals. Before I gained consciousness around my consumer choices I would often consume things in a dim-witted, distracted state of awareness and choose movies or novels based on convenience or advertisements and even sometimes repeat statements without giving them much thought.

By devoting myself to my yoga practice I began to break away from the distraction of consumerism and see endless possibilities for a peaceful life. How I felt on the inside was and remains what mattered. Attraction changed from something associated with material things to a powerful force that emanated from basic self-confidence that, in and of itself, created a beauty that I could see, feel and enjoy.

Yoga is at its deepest level the search for inner peace. By definition yoga means union and when you are searching for peace this union must remain with you on all levels. It is when you feel a deep sense of peace and acceptance for who you really are that your beauty shines forth and glows from within. One of the first tenets of yoga philosophy that helps practitioners move into a deeper relationship with themselves is the teaching of non-attachment, or in Sanskrit aparigraha. As you release the emotional clinging for various objects, success, relationships and states of being you begin a purification process that involves a shift in perception, behavior and vibration.

One of the paths towards peace involves letting go of the emotional hook for various objects, states of being and emotions. Like a dramatic cleansing process, the experience of going to practice yoga with Guruji and Sharath, along with living life in India, offered me a forum to integrate a first person experience and understanding of what it meant to live without getting stuck in the rut of getting exactly what I wanted when I wanted it and how I wanted it.

This was particularly challenging for me as I can sometimes be very addicted to the ability to control the outcome of my life experience. Of course, I slowly began to realize that when I fell into the habit of controlling outcomes, I also cut myself off from allowing life to happen around me. By attempting to outsource my problems and buy my way in and out of situations I was also controlling my experience of life a little too tightly. In the practice of yoga one of the most essential lessons learned is that there is no quick fix solution. In order to feel the kind of release that leads to peace I had to face myself in all the places where I felt ugly and learn to respond to those places with acceptance and peace. During practice with my two Indian teachers there was no way out. I had to face exactly where I was in practice, my mind and my life. I could not beg, borrow, buy, outsource, fake, blow over, throw smoke at or cheat my way around the reality of yoga. I was either doing it correctly or not. I was either ready for the next posture or not. I was not the one who got to choose. Sri K. Pattabhi Jois was my teacher and he gave me the strength, faith and courage to face myself as I never had before. During long days in Mysore when the hours felt like years I gained the courage to face myself in all states.

In order for me to live a balanced life I needed to find myself amid the life I had been inadvertently living. I began the work of inner growth every morning on an interwoven network of cotton rugs in the Old Shala in Mysore under Jois's guidance. While Western studios often have perfectly laid hardwood floors, four uneven rugs layered over each other in a network mesh that created deep ridges of raised points. Twelve people were jammed into the space where four would fit comfortably by American standards. There were only inches between each mat. Hands clashed, shoulder touched, smells inhabited every corner of the room, and Guruji and Sharath's eyes were on everyone. There was no room to escape and plenty of fodder for the egocentric mind.

During this period of time yoga consumed my life. I lived, breathed, ate, drank and slept yoga. At night I dreamt my way into new yoga postures I had never seen before and took the inspiration to my mat the following day. I awoke ten minutes before my alarm for the first time in my life, refreshed from sleep and ready for the day. One fitful morning I had loads of extra energy and funneled it straight into my yoga routine. I did everything to an extreme. From the first breathe of what is called the Sun Salutation, or Surya Namaskara, I looked up at my fingers and knew that I was greeting a new chapter in my life. I lifted and reached not just from the physical level but from the deepest part of my soul. I was desperate, longing, yearning and dying to have my heart taken by yoga. While I certainly felt better after spending nearly six weeks bending, breathing, twisting and lifting my body in yoga postures I did not feel totally, one hundred percent at peace. So I decided to ask my newly found eighty-five year old yoga master Sri K. Pattabhi Jois where to really find it. The kind of availability that Jois allowed his students at the Old Shala is rare gift among such highly esteemed teachers. Every day of the week except Saturday he sat in the foyer of his building and invited all of his students to ask questions. Most people in a position of power guard their privacy, time and space with fierce boundaries. He was wide open. When I crowded into the small space where approximately twenty-five yoga students gathered that afternoon I called him "Guruji" in earnest.

The moist afternoon air held the room in its heavy, swollen thickness. Cutting the air with a languid spin, the cheap white plastic of the ceiling fan tinkered on the edge of falling down. All eyes were pointed at the grandfatherly Guruji reading his afternoon paper in the local dialect of Kanada. The room held its breath. The race of my mind formed the words of a question that sat heavy and urgent while awaiting delivery, hanging onto my tongue and tickling the roof my mouth. My heart was swollen. The burning desire of the moment's immediacy magnified the afternoon heat and I was sweating. I felt like I had literally handed my heart and my faith over to the capable arms of my teacher.

"Guruji, where can I find the inner peace?"

Rumpling his newspaper, he coughed and sat up straighter to look me straight in the eye. My heart skipped a beat. He barked back, "What?"

When I am nervous my speech pattern quickens and registers in at five hundred words per minute. Native English speakers often cannot follow my train of thought, let alone this aging Guru. Yet somehow he did manage to understand me, after a second try. There is something that happens when you have the desire to put everything out there in one instant and in these moments speech itself often impedes communication. While I prayed for a direct pipeline into the heart of my teacher, I simply repeated the words again, this time with a careful slowness to account for language, culture and age.

"Guruji, where can I find inner peace?"

Wearing the traditional outfit of South Indian Brahmins, a white piece of thin cotton with gold edging called a loongi and a Western loose-fitting yoga tank top, this man, my teacher, gave me the gift of his full attention. He could have waved off the question as being naive, coming from a crazy female Westerner with a shaved head and piercings in the wrong places who had been doing yoga seriously less than a year. But he took me seriously. And my question was indeed earnest. I did desperately want to find inner peace and that was my reason for starting yoga. My desire had remained unspoken throughout my life until the moment I uttered those words in his presence. As I gazed back at Guruji he was all I saw.

He said, "You take practice. One style of yoga, one teacher many years. You do three things: posture, looking and breathing. Then Shantih is coming, no problem."

After completing his response, he paused and studied me, holding me in his gaze he said everything once more. He didn't raise his voice or gush with emotion. His presence was calm, steady, clear and to the point, perhaps a great manifestation of a strong steady mind. It contained the essence and simplicity of how he taught. There was no flowering verbiage from angels or demons hidden from the world. Instead, the answer lied in practice, filled with the fruits of one's daily devotion, one's very own sweat, spice and soul. And there was a teacher who always saw every one of his students exactly where they really were. After that afternoon I had faith in my own ability to make peace with myself through the technique of yoga. The most powerful words are not necessarily new words. They are the ones spoken from the lips of a person whom we can finally believe in, a person whose integrity is unquestionable and a person whose very being inspires greatness.

In my experience Guruji always spoke directly to the truth of exactly where a student was emotionally and spiritually. He had this uncanny knack for addressing the deeper nature of the person asking the question so his answers were not always related directly to what the questioner had in mind. He was never a man of many words, especially in the English language, and always gave a simple answer that doubled as a Zen koan (puzzle) to solve over the course of your lifetime. His answers came straight from the heart and spoke to a long sleeping place inside of me. I didn't realize it at the time, but that moment transformed my very being and it is one that I drew upon repeatedly in my own teaching.

Even though Guruji did not say anything that I had not heard before, his presence combined with the words he did say were enough to inspire me to delve into the heart of yoga. When I walked away from conference that afternoon I was also struck with another hard truth. I realized that my mere presence in India was not going to make me peaceful. Buying a ticket to a foreign country to twist and bend myself was not a panacea for every problem I felt. Instead, I began to realize it was going to be the hard work done in subtle moments of quietude that would lead towards the realization of real, lasting peace. Yoga gives you the courage to choose a more peaceful life in each moment of your day if you can unearth the ability to believe in yourself every step of the way. The practice of yoga harnesses the power of the mind and gives you access to its true inner power. Yoga essentially amplifies the power of the mind and increases its capacity for concentrated focus. This heightened focus allows you to be more successful at devoting yourself to particular life goals. Yoga teaches you how to be humble and willing to put in the work required to achieve the results that you want. When you unroll your mat and commit to the total journey of yoga you unlock the mind's power to transform physical substance with the power of spirit. With practice, this is exactly what I learned how to do.

CHAPTER FOUR
LOVE AND INDIA

Along with hard work, my second trip to India was about love—love of myself, falling in love, loving India, and understanding the deeper nature of love. I knew that I would return to Mysore to spend time with my teacher but wanted an adventure too. And so I bought an around the world aeroplane ticket that took me to India through Kuwait City right around the time of the Iraq War.

The journey began quietly on an empty plane from JFK to Kuwait City. Then enroute to Trivandrum Airport, close to Kovalam Beach in India, I noticed another pair of blue eyes on the flight. He was the only other Westerner and his unfortunate seat in front of the bathroom, at the very rear edge of the rows of passengers, made it easy for me to turn my head and steal a glimpse. In a sea of turbans and Hindus we stood out just a little. He came from Copenhagen, via Frankfurt. I came from Miami, via New York. While he was shoved in the back row, I had room enough for a spare seat and slept most of the six-hour flight.

The early hours of dawn greeted our landing in nearly pitch-blackness; the tops of swaying palm trees lined the perimeter of the airport. Trivandrum airport is less developed than Bangalore airport. It's an Indian city in the midst of rain forest vegetation near a stretch of beach. Yes, planes land and take off from here. Yes they have customs officials who stamp your passport. Yes you even have a baggage claim area. But airport to me always implies a high level of development, lines, orders, officiating members of various military or guarding services, the bright air-conditioned halls of airline check-ins. Trivandrum airport is more like a concrete landing strip with an attached bunker for pick up, drop up and general delivery. I don't remember there being a kiosk of any sort, but perhaps I was just too tired to notice. More infested by the salty air of the ocean than Bangalore, when you land here you almost sense the vacationer's restless time off hanging in the air.

A destination for both Indian and international tourists,

Kovalam Beach is India's version of a small, secluded tourist town. Complete with fruits salads, coconuts, a German Bakery, sunglass shops, cheesy mementos, and ocean view hotels, it attracts a transient crowd. Further south and therefore hotter, it's unbearable during the summer season; the blistering, butchering heat slays you with its mere persistence. Ominously held within every winter's sunny day is a fear of summer. Stay in this Lonely Planet guidebook destination just a week too long and the mosquitoes, heat and humidity will torture you until you surrender to purchasing a flight out the next day.

I arrived to winter's mild heat as I disembarked the plane. Standing on the jet way, its concrete slab poured across the jungle floor, I boarded a bus that dropped me off at the airport bunker. Ushered through customs lines and into a waiting area, I entered baggage claim where we met, face to face. At six feet tall his elegantly long limbs fell in baggy jean pockets, and an angular jaw line etched into his chiseled frame which made his blue eyes beam brightly as he looked straight into my eyes.

"Hey, are you doing that yoga thing?" came out of me before I could second-guess myself.

"Eh, yeah," he answered, travel groggy but nonplussed just the same.

"Do you want to share a taxi?" I questioned, not because it was love at first sight, but because I thought it might be better for two lost fools to figure out where they were going rather than just one.

"Sure, I've been here before. I know where I'm going. Do you have any bags?" he asked.

"Yeah, I have to get them. Do you mind waiting?"

He didn't. We waited together and introduced ourselves, shook hands, and spoke about our journeys thus far. His name was Tim, he was from Denmark, and he said an Indian man had talked his ear off during the flight to the extent of asking him to get him a work visa to Denmark. Tim made me smile and laugh right away.

In the grayish white ambassador that doubles for a taxi in India we sat in the backseat together. I liked him already. I told myself to settle down, that he was the first person that I met in India and the purpose of this trip was all about me, not about the attractive stranger I was staring at in the backseat of a car. Later I discovered that, in that moment, he too was harboring the same attractions and reservations. But here we were, the responsible golden-hearted man from northern Europe with the irresponsible would-be party-girl graduate student, turned spiritual seeker, with no direction in her life, except for Mysore, of course. We both sat there nurturing a one-hour old attraction, keeping it at bay with logic, reason and restraint.

A day too early for yoga we two strangers found ourselves stranded on a preseason Indian beach town with nothing to do. I suggested a swim in the ocean and then we both agreed to have breakfast after. With rooms already reserved, bags dropped at hotels and a hunger for food and for each other setting in, we took to the beach. The shoreline sparkled in the early daylight hours. Fisherman, street vendors and beach goers were either sleeping or eating. We stood there, alone, on the brown, black, muddy coloured sandy beach with palm trees stretched out in every direction. The glowing orb of the sun loomed behind the palm fronds, silhouetting the skyline with spiky edges, poking holes in the blue above. Brown and cream spotted shells lined the beach, teeming with life. Miniscule fish pecked at the offerings. We walked into a picture perfect day. Sea spray lapped at our feet and we entered the water. Barely cool waves poured over us as we wordlessly flirted, averting our eyes.

Over the next five weeks a romance took over our lives. We lived, breathed and drank each other every chance we got. His steady strength, good intentions, honesty, will and beautiful spirit drew me in. One night he said to me that he wanted to know who I really was, that he wanted to really know me deeply. I had no idea what to do with this. I was good at love affairs but had never really got to know anyone. I did not want a relationship, I could barely tolerate a lover. He walked me home one night, kissed me on the cheek. I have no memory of what we said, I only remember that my knees got weak when he left. I was in love and didn't know it. No, that's not true. I was in love and didn't dare to admit it to myself.

Five weeks passed in a blur and now he was scheduled to leave; he was a choreographer, had his own company, his own life and his own country to return to. As for me, the next six months of my life would be about Mysore.

The night he left I slept on his bed. I was too sleepy, too afraid to admit my feelings. The next day he said goodbye, that he would write me, call me, we would be in touch. A strong man with a soft heart, tears flowed over his cheeks onto mine. The ambassador was waiting, his plane was leaving, he had to go. I watched the car drive away. Sometimes love hits you over the head at all the wrong moments. You may run from it but sooner or later you've got to answer the gentle, yet persistent knocking at the door of your soul.

When Tim left my world collapsed. I missed him and loved him but somehow I also did not feel that I had a right to my feelings. As he lingered on my body and in my heart I sent an email to Denmark that was both reserved and open. We had no intention of really seeing each other again so I felt that any contact was suspect. But I dreamed of traveling to Mysore with him, sharing every step of the journey. Three very long, sad days after he left I got an email back that ended any reservation and brought a smile back to my face. Just that he wrote to me was enough. The actual words only confirmed what I already knew, that his feelings were deep and true. In his short sentences I could hear his Danish cadence saying that he missed me more than he ever thought possible and that his feelings ran deep. My heart had found a home although my body was about to travel to Mysore once more.

* * *

One week later marked the opening of the "New Shala" in Mysore. I arrived alone to the home for Ashtanga Yoga, the same place I visited before only it wasn't as familiar. New marble flooring opened onto a ballroom size yoga shala, holding eight extra large red-yellow-blue-white Indian style thick woven cotton canvas rugs in one, very large yoga space. I had been one of the first students to practice here and now there was so much space that people from the Old Shala didn't really know what to make of it. There were no ridges in the rugs. There were more fluorescent lights than anyone really needed at five in the morning. There were more students than anyone ever thought possible to teach at once. Everything that I had loved about the Old Shala was gone and now there were questions, concerns, anticipation and wide staring eyes.

Having arrived one week after the consecration ceremony to bless the space, I first traversed this maze of new construction with gaping eyes. I devoured the newness of it all, ready to make new memories in the New Shala. I was young and ready to plow ahead. Straight off the plane from Kovalam Beach into the heart of Ashtanga Yoga, I dropped off my bags at a very dodgy local hotel that I would not recommend to anyone and walked over to see my teachers.

Meandering through a sea of flip-flops that guarded the steps, I hopped, jumped and nearly fell straight into the lobby. As I entered Guruji popped his head out of the practice room. Holding onto an edge of the doorframe that sectioned off the practice space from the lobby space, he stared me straight in the eye and said, "You come? Practice?" He glowed. He wore a large white tank top and shorts. He was barefoot. I immediately wished I had arrived five months earlier. I was overflowing with gratitude to be in Mysore again with my teacher. Being the emotional wreck that I was, I almost cried. I was on my knees, hands touching his feet, saying, "Yes, Guruji. Thank you Guruji." As I crawled to my feet, his outstretched hands pulled me for a welcoming hug and kiss on the lips. After the greeting, he said, "MMM. Good. You start tomorrow." A moment later his presence vanished back into the room of yogis. His illuminated smile and casual friendliness made me think of Ganesh, the elephant deity. The journey into the heart would only deepen on this trip as I already felt more alive at my spiritual center. I prayed for the grace to remove any obstacles along my path.

Then, on my way out I noticed the greater presence of a second individual. His name was Sharath Rangaswamy and he was a teacher who tended the yoga garden his grandfather built held a high standard for all Mysore students. He had eyes like a tiger—younger, more judicious—and skinny legs that betrayed his superhuman strength and also left lycra shorts hanging loose. I remembered how his delicate hands could coax one's body into postures with very little effort, just a light touch and persistence. Just like his grandfather he has a presence that watches when you think he's not aware. Like his grandfather he would not let a student slide by on any posture and also like his grandfather, you did not want to make him mad at you. He was also someone you could easily love to pieces.

Sharah's eyes met mine and he said, "When you came?"

"Just now," I replied.

"You take registration today afternoon, start practice tomorrow, 6 AM."

"Congratulations on the New Shala, it's beautiful," I offered as my hands slid into prayer. I turned my eyes downward and in a mild bow, walked away.

* * *

Having no housing arranged, no pre-ordered taxi and no friend to welcome me, I began the search for an apartment. The hotel I found myself in for two horrible nights was by far the worst place I have ever stayed. With no running water, grey plaid sheets, brick red bathroom flooring and a self-flushing Indian toilet littered with flies, I wanted out fast. Mind you the place was clean, the rooms were tended to, and the staff were nice, but there is only so much you can do without gutting a place and starting over.

The first day in Mysore is usually always a scramble to find housing, change money, make friends, eat curries and drink coconuts. This was no exception. I walked into a small enclave in a series of shops on what's called "Gokulam Main Street". There I found a sign that indicated there was a real estate agent at work. Inside I noted a few plastic chairs, one black rotary telephone, a few files and six Indian men standing in a cream colored space the size of a closet. The only insignia outfitted was a hand painted sign above the entry that said "Broker". I walked up to one of the only females in the room—she had trusting eyes.

"Hello, are you a real estate agent here?" I queried.

"Yes, what you want?"

The reply came from a large-bellied man in an orange plaid shirt behind the desk on one of the only plastic chairs.

I gulped and then managed, "I want an apartment for four months in the Gokulam area."

"How much do you want to pay?"

"Not more than 4,000 rupees." This was then the equivalent of about eighty dollars. I was on a bit of a budget, with no income, and hoped to stay a while. Luckily there was no credit check, no background search, just a simple question.

"You wait, ten minutes. We go see."

I waited while the real estate agent made phone calls and drank more chai. I joined in and drank two chai myself. Chai in India is not chai in the West. Starbucks and copycat coffee chains have sweetened and syruped the chai right out of chai. It really just means tea with milk in small mini-glasses served piping hot with equal parts sugar. Maybe a little more sugar. I learned quickly to order "sugarless chai" and then add my own sugar after.

The large-bellied man exited the enclosure of this office motioning for me to follow, and we were off. We saw three apartments and I took the third for the whopping price of 2,000 rupees a month, just under fifty U.S. dollars. It was a small two bedroom flat on the very outskirts of Gokulam and had a wraparound balcony, a kitchen and an Indian bathroom. There was only one problem—no hot water. Well, not exactly no hot water. The old Indian system for hot water was to boil it yourself by burning discarded coconut shells. Not really up for this method we agreed that the landlord would raise the monthly rental by 500 rupees and I would pay a refundable deposit of 4,000 and a large 25-gallon hot water electrical heater would be installed the next day. The landlord also suggested that he arrange for his maid to come every other day to clean my little flat for a fee of 250 rupees a month. I agreed, we shook hands, exchanged money and within twenty-four hours of my arrival I had rented my first apartment in Mysore.

Arriving in Mysore as a now twenty-five year old solitary female traveler, I braved the elements of chance. I sorted it out when I got there. It was a lesson in learning how to trust the experience itself without planning and controlling every little detail. Sitting in my new apartment I realized one small error of oversight; I rented a flat, but I had no furniture. I had a bedroom and no bed. I had a kitchen and no utensils. I had a bathroom and nothing in it. The solution—I went shopping.

With the aid of a rickshaw driver for transportation and guidance I purchased a mattress, pots, pans, knives, spoons, forks, buckets for flushing, buckets for showering, buckets for cleaning, carpets, hangers, and numerous other items I deemed necessary for my survival in the outback. On this trip my small apartment suffered heat waves, mosquito infestations, power outages, water cuts, beggar children knocking at the door, and various other things that I now have a mind to ask about before renting a flat. Needless to say, I survived. On my first night I settled into my new apartment, fell asleep amid over-excitement about practice the next morning. The only thing missing was the person whose arms I desperately wanted to feel around me.

* * *

Daily life in Mysore can be very simple which is both good and bad. Unless you have a project to occupy your time, there is a tendency to mull over things a bit too much. As a dedicated yogi I was attempting to train my mind to remain one pointed and yet every spare moment was spent dreaming of Tim. I wondered how his day was, what his life was like in Copenhagen. I thought of trying to find a working internet café where I might email him, and endlessly wondered when we might speak again. I was preoccupied with thoughts of his love. In fact, the only time that I didn't have Tim on my mind was during practice at the New Shala.

The Ashtanga Yoga Nilayam in Lakshmipuram where I practiced before was now called the Old Shala and the new building where I practiced in Gokulam was the New Shala. The New Shala was housed in a compound where Guruji, Sharath, Saraswati (Guruji's daughter and Sharath's mother) and their families lived. Rather than a small walk-up of eight steps, there was almost a full floor that lifted the New Shala from the street. With a weaving network of double steps the entryway appeared more like an M.C. Escher painting than a mere doorway. Large, dark honey-colored, high gloss varnished wooden doors, marked with new gold fixtures, locks and handles separated the outside from the inside in a much more clearly defined fashion. Inside polished white marble tiles greeted me in the lobby and waiting area.

Although I'd been advancing in my personal yoga practice during my time away, I had been doing so without the supervision of a teacher. I practiced alone primarily, played around with friends occasionally and figured out for myself when I might be ready to try something new. I relished the private space of self-practice and yet here I was in a space of fifty-plus people at a time, in a city with nearly 150 yoga students.

I entered the New Shala with my own delusions of grandeur. Having been in Mysore before I at least knew not to proclaim my ideas of greatness to my teachers, but I held them close to my heart, at bay from free expression. I decided to hunker down and actively practice accepting not getting what I wanted and getting what I did not want. My head hung low and I did my best to practice acceptance, patience and not beat myself up about it. My typical fashion would be to blame myself for not coming back to Mysore soon enough or to pity myself for not starting earlier, or even wish I could devote more to India and live there for three years as some students do. And yet this trip, in particular, led me down the road towards self-love and self-acceptance.

One day Sharath came over and told me to do the first two postures of Intermediate Series. He watched, said nothing and then walked away. Rather than being grateful for starting to move forward, I was immediately filled with an incredible resistance at the idea of learning each posture of the Intermediate over again, one-by-one. I didn't know what I was expecting, but I got depressed instantly. Not only was I attached to the practice I had developed over the last year, but I also wanted to be further along in the Series than I was and basically be anywhere other than where I was. With incredible resistance to my reality, I began fighting it internally. For Sunday, Monday and Tuesday I practiced the Primary Series and the first two postures of the Intermediate Series with much chagrin and a big attitude.

Slowly I began to learn that yoga's deeper lesson teaches dedicated practitioners that they are okay regardless of what posture they're doing. Rather than using the postures to give people a sense of self-worth, yoga offers the notion that people themselves are already worthy and perfect. Instead of expecting more advanced postures to save you from yourself, the real lesson is learning how to accept and love yourself as you are. For me this was no easy task.

After struggling in my intermediate postures I surrendered and finally began to enter the lobby of the New Shala willing to learn, relearn and do whatever it was going to take. I somehow managed to give up my ambition and turn it over to my teachers. On that very day all the physical postures flowed with grace and ease. Guruji and Sharath let me do something unthinkable–they taught me the remaining 36 postures to complete the Intermediate Series in one day. It might seem obvious to the outside eye that the only sensible thing to do when you fly half way around the world, live in a foreign country and pay high fees to practice yoga is to surrender to what the teachers want you to do. But far from the case many people come to show Guruji and Sharath what they can do, and I was one of them. I tried to use Mysore for my own twisted sense of approval and through that ego-driven struggle I learned how to let go of my hubris. It's often the case that the greatest teaching has nothing to do with how you do a certain posture, it's more often a lesson of the mind that changes deeply held belief patterns.

For nearly three weeks I worked on this same practice with varying degrees of help from Guruji and Sharath. My teachers were not verbal instructors, instead they taught with their presence, in a way outside the normal region of logic. Every day during my practice when I wanted their help, they left me alone. Every day when I was off in a dreamland, they yelled at me and brought me back down to reality. Every day when I wanted to be left alone, they were in my face. I learned to relax and let go.

* * *

The Ashtanga Yoga method works in a non-linear way. Sometimes you perform deep postures only to have sleeping memories stirred up and revisit your consciousness later during the day. Sometimes you find yourself confronted with memories and emotions in the midst of practice. On one weekend in March during the third month of my second trip to India I found myself facing one of the most difficult patterns in my life. I had been thinking of the possibility of being in a loving, committed relationship with Tim, something I had not even dared to dream before. I began to ruminate on my past relationships and question the reason behind their failure.

Then suddenly it was hot in Mysore, but I was freezing. My yoga teachers Guruji and Sharath had given us a particularly long holiday weekend. In Ashtanga yoga there is no practice on the full and the new moon. Dedicated students such as myself come to love these mandatory days off and the rest could not have come at a more perfect moment for me. Thursday evening a fever set in and I was sick and shivering. Covered in a cold sweat and unable to sleep, I drank a ginger lemon honey concoction and hoped my body would heal. Not only was I experiencing a violent fever and achy pains in every joint, but my mind was in the midst of a storm. I was feeling depressed, overwhelmed and dizzy. In an effort to escape the mental onslaught I listened to the Icelandic sounds of Sigur Ros on my iPod. I slowly surrendered to the music and a gateway into my forgotten memory opened. As each song reached its crescendo my mind was transported back through panoramic views of my own past. I saw my life as I had never seen it before—not only through the eyes of my experience, but through the eyes of the deepest wisdom possible. What I saw changed my life forever.

The wavy coloured multi-dimensionality of the whole experience haunts me to this day. As these powerful memories surfaced I was surrounded by sounds, colours and feelings. With both a bird's eye view and a roundabout perspective that included all parties involved, I witnessed the foundations of every relationship I had ever had. Step by step I retraced, relived and re-experienced these relationships and felt my own feelings in the matter, but in an entirely new way. Rather than merely reenacting the same old lies about how wonderful it all was or about how nice I was, I saw the truth in every single interaction. Like a thread that linked each separate relationship together I saw the fundamental act of dishonesty that I had engaged in. I had not entered into a single relationship out of a genuine desire to be with the other person. This cycle of suffering stemmed from an inability to love myself deeply.

At this stark realization I woke enveloped in a sadness unlike any I had known before. My hands were interlocked as I cried and I suddenly released my grip and allowed my fingers to move freely. And as I did a warm, golden white light burst into my room and the misery was transformed into awareness by the clear light of consciousness. I am not sure if I believed in the possibility of such a transcendental experience, but both the memory and the experience have stayed with me since. I have often read with wonder about the power of spiritual breakthroughs and doubted their veracity. Yet here I was in the middle of my own realization that defied the normal bounds of possibility. It was like logic, reason, gravity, time and space all vanished to reveal the true nature of being under the illusion of reality. There is no other way to describe this than that the presence of God filled the room. I felt immediately totally and completely at home in my skin. Not that I had not felt good about myself or enjoyed my body, but that the spirit of myself now felt comfortable in residence within my body. I understood instantly the power of tapping into the pure potential of spiritual awareness. I understood the nature of love, the pulse of the universe underneath and infused into every living creature. Everywhere I looked was new, fresh and alive. The walls glowed, the floor was blessed, the ceiling was hallowed. It was not a relaxing peace that silenced a long shout, but instead was a resounding joy that echoed in the mountains of infinity. Peace and beauty stood like towering giants in every corner of the room. Attentive, alert and alive, I met them with laughter and freedom. It was three in the morning when I had the urge to go to the bathroom. I filled a bucket with water. Suddenly no longer feverish, no longer filled with physical pain, I stood naked, bright-eyed and awake and I poured the cold water over my head while saying aloud to myself, "With this water, I thee cleanse". And in that moment my life changed. I have no idea where these words came from; it almost felt as though they were being spoken through me, as though a power greater than me was taking root in my body. Maybe this was the answer to my prayers, a moment of grace. I didn't see Ganesh, but in the sacred space of transformation I washed away the dirt of the past and stepped into the dawn of a new day.

It should be said that I have never considered myself a Christian in any traditional sense. I feel more like a Buddhist in terms of philosophical orientation and take after my Japanese, Buddhist grandfather. I practice yoga but am certainly not a Hindu though I love Sanskrit and respect the Indian deities. Yet in my most personally spiritual moments I have always felt a sense of God that unites all beings in the universe. The presence I feel is not religious, but spiritual. The terminology that comes out of my mouth sometimes contains Christian undertones. A basic tenet of yoga is surrender and as far as I understand surrender, it is also a Christian value as well. In this healing moment in Mysore I learned the deeper definition of surrender along the spiritual path.

When I showed up in the shala to practice again everything felt restored to a state of innocence. Initially I felt the change resonate deeply within me but soon afterwards realized there was much work to be done. Just because I shifted did not necessary mean that the rest of my life had shifted as well. This one realization meant years of work unraveling and healing long established patterns of being, relating and interacting in the world. Epiphany moments are not ends in themselves. They open a door for you to walk through with your own strength, power and resolution.

One thing was clear, however: I was finally able and ready to share love with another. I remember reading an email from Tim where he told me for the first time that he loved me. I waited five minutes for Yahoo! Mail to open, then another five to get to my inbox and a desperate final few before his email popped up on the computer screen. I scrolled down, hungrily, riveted by every word. I could hear his voice and feel his heart. I also felt my love. I wrote back quickly, excitedly, and told him that I loved him too.

R. Sharath Jois helping Kino MacGregor in backbending in Mysore.

Sri K. Pattabhi Jois & Kino MacGregor in Mysore.

Kino practicing in India.

Yoga Dandasana in India.

Tim Feldmann & Kino MacGregor in Mysore.

Tim Feldmann & Kino MacGregor practicing in India.

Guruji & Sharath in the Old Shala in Mysore
(photo by Govinda Kai).

Kino MacGregor & Tim Feldmann during guided second series with Guruji.

Kino with Guruji in Mysore.

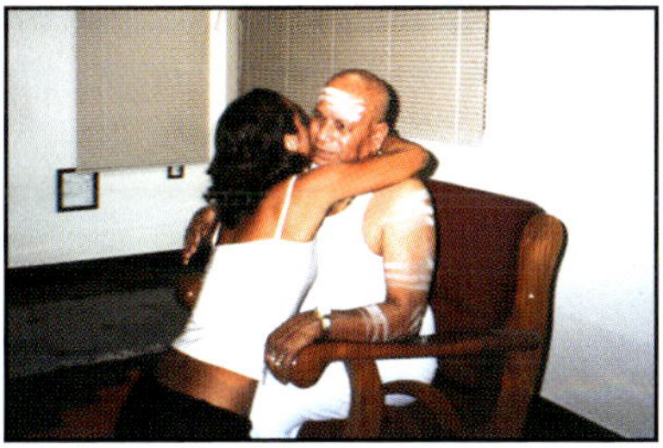

The streets of Mysore.

Kino, Tim & Guruji in Mysore.

Padmasana at Miami Life Center.

Outside the Old Shala in Lakhsmipuram, Mysore.

Kino at the Old Shala in Lakhsmipuram, Mysore.

Bairavasana at Miami Life Center.

Miami Beach.

CHAPTER FIVE
THE HEALED BODY

In the grey concrete walls of my parents' garage I unrolled an extra-thick black yoga mat. Holding onto the thread of my teacher Sri K. Pattabhi Jois I began my daily practice of twisting, turning and breathing in a private, candle-lit ceremony. Since my first visit to Mysore I had practiced primarily on my own without a daily teacher and this made me stronger and more responsible. While many people love the guidance of a group session, I loved the privacy of true self-practice. Without the teacher's gaze I found the freedom to look like a complete fool, try ridiculous methods, repeat things ten times and fall without injuring my neighbors. Discipline was easy. Yoga began to fill the void left open for so many years. I allowed yoga to trade sadness for joy, exchange heartbreak for happiness and swap loss of self-confidence for the seed of a genuine sense of self.

While I began to excel in the physicality of its poses I was still green in the area of daily meditation. Six days a week I sat cross-legged and followed my breath, trying unsuccessfully to keep my attention on one point for between five to twenty minutes. That small amount of time was all I could handle before the inside world of my mind started going stark raving mad. I was barely home a few weeks before I got the idea to go to Nepal. It was June 2003 and I didn't feel ready to be back in Miami yet. Yoga had led me to the inner door and now I couldn't turn away. I wanted to learn how to use meditation to take me deeper. And so I booked another plane ticket.

In the foothills of the Himalayas just outside Katmandu I entered into a Ten Day Silent Meditation Retreat after spending six months in India studying Ashtanga yoga. Called Vipassana meditation this technique is taught in the tradition of S.N. Goenka at centers all around the world. I agreed, as all participants do, to maintain noble silence, eat a vegetarian diet, stay within the retreat center's ground, abide by the center's monastic timetables, abstain from violence, stealing, lying, sexual activity and adornments like jewellery for the duration of the retreat. In exchange I entered into a sacred space that was undisturbed by modern life and received a truly transformational teaching for whatever monetary donation I could afford to give at the completion of the course. All centers are donation based and self-sustaining, meaning that donations from one course pay for the following course and keep everything going without the need to charge students a set fee. The teachers offer their services for free as well and give their time to benefit students without asking anything in return. Joining this Vipassana meditation retreat was like a meditation crash course for adventurous dummies. I got everything dumped onto me in one go. I lived a monastic life with pure, ate only sattvic (think healthy, bland and vegetarian) food, practiced ancient meditation techniques, accepted the charity of others and rose in the middle of the night for spiritual practice. It was nothing short than a life changing experience and perhaps the best ten days of my life.

When I entered the Vipassana retreat I had nothing but a full cup for what meditation would be. I thought I would see the auric field, communicate with angels, awaken my chakras, stimulate my kundalini and visualize sacred symbols. Instead I just sat there and focused on the breath. I grew exceedingly bored. Rather than fancy lights, drama and the whole Broadway show of spirituality arriving and tapping me on the shoulder, I got only the breath. With continual non-stop practice for five days I was able to maintain my attention on this single point of attention for intervals in excess of one full minute without losing my mind. It is sometimes excruciatingly boring and other times unbelievably interesting to hold your attention on your breath. The mere point of focus is like a holiday from life's anxieties. I felt constricted between the expansive field of consciousness and a claustrophobia that wanted nothing more than to escape into a triple latte, a movie and a chocolate bar. But the breath never left me. It stayed and waited for my claustrophobia to subside. Five days into the retreat, after nearly fifty hours of sitting, something settled. I guess you could say it was my busy mind, but it felt like something deeper.

Just as I was getting into the groove on this Vipassana

meditation boot camp I was instructed to direct my undivided attention to the internal world of my body. Rather that just focus on the breath I was now advised to scan my body, part by part, with the same internal focus. In a sense I was being asked to listen to my body as I had learned to listen to the breath. I had never learned how to really pay attention to my body. While super models were standards for apparent physical beauty I never treated my body as an intelligent living being with wisdom to share. Sports and exercise asked the body to perform, placing feeling and health second to results and aesthetics. Yet during the Vipassana retreat the main attention given to my body was intended to help me learn to listen and respect the messages I received. Although I started feeling my body through yoga, I didn't necessarily understand what it was saying. I had always asked my body to be something—thin, beautiful, sexy, flexible, strong or cool. But I had never asked my body what it wanted to do, how it felt or what was going on inside. In essence, I had never really made friends with my body. Instead I had used my body for various purposes without taking the time to build a loving, heartfelt relationship with it. With calm, attentive focus I drew my awareness and concentration from the tip of my head downwards and covered the entire span of my body, inside and out without any achievement in mind.

Working my way through this inner world was deep and intense. I felt the being inside my own skin and I realized that in some sense I had been running away from her my whole life. This shifting point of awareness culminated to a breaking point the moment that my attention landed on my upper left thigh. Having scanned my body, part by part, piece by piece I discovered that this was the area that I had never admired. When I directed my mind to be with my left thigh sadness overcame me. I began to realize that I stored negative thoughts about my body in exactly all the places that I trained myself to dislike. From the time I was twelve I avoided looking at my thighs and this routine stayed with me until I went on the Vipassana retreat at twenty-five. There I realized that I carried a disappointment in my shape that manifested in the exact thing I wanted to change—extra pounds stored on my thighs. For the first time I observed and listened to my body with no desire to change it. The clean light of awareness washed away years of muck and mud that clouded my perception. Never again have I felt the same punitive eyes of judgment look at my body or the body of another. This is not to say that I never feel uncomfortable or a little plumper than I would like. Just like anyone else I have days where I feel like I'm carrying an extra bit of weight but the sense of embarrassment over a part of my body is essentially gone. In its place is a feeling of love for my body and soul, for the gift that it is and the beauty that it radiates.

Still it is interesting how I had so negatively judged my body in the past and how this was intrinsically connected to my sense of self-esteem. I always thought of my body in terms of good and bad. I could only criticize my body when I felt separate from it and yet, in truth, the body and mind are united in their expression of the inner being. There is a far deeper and more profound level of unification possible between the seemingly multi-faceted aspects of oneself.

In my case, I believe this depth of awareness came for me during a Vipassana retreat because I brought these hidden assumptions about my body to my yoga practice. While yoga also teaches that, the mind and body are one deeply connected matrix, I could only experience the teaching to the degree that I allowed. In the beginning I blamed my body for the time it took to learn various postures but after I completed my first Vipassana retreat I was somehow free of the self-limiting disbelief in my body's potential. I began to respect the notion that things take the time they take. No amount of self-hating, self-denigration, self punishment, jealousy, bargaining, faking or anger can change that.

Of course, to come to this understanding I had to integrate the realizations I experienced during meditation with daily yoga practice. I began applying the loving attitude towards myself that I learned during Vipassana meditation. Yoga became a listening and being practice rather than a doing and achieving practice. I could no longer lie to myself about how I was really feeling. With daily yoga practice in this method I began a slow re-education of my mind and body that undid the damage done by years of a rigid belief in a stark separation between mind and body.

* * *

My travel home was long—Nepal to Taipei, Taipei to L.A. and finally L.A. to Miami. The first thing I wanted to do when I got back to the U.S. was call Tim. I dreamt of him during the Vipassana and knew that I needed to see him again. I felt like a new person and I wanted to share that with him, but my layover in L.A. wasn't long enough. By the time I arrived home to Miami the time difference was too distant. He would have been asleep, so I sent another email, this time from a fast and perky American Wi-Fi.

After I returned from Nepal I read Dr. Candace Pert's book titled, Your Body is Your Subconscious Mind which explores this topic with careful attention to scientific validity. I learned how biology has wisdom deep within every living cell and how it is only when the body and mind act in harmony and make peace with themselves that true serenity is possible. One of the goals of yoga practice is to create a forum for practitioners where they can directly experience the unity of the body and mind.

Back in Miami I fought to resist the lifestyle I knew before yoga. I began to study the outside, the realm of mind and matter and how every living creature is in constant dialogue with the realm of spirit, co-creating entire worlds, lives and realities. I came to believe that the spirit is a constant whisper of the infinite that works towards establishing peace and harmony in one's being. I was tempted to replace the duality between the body and the mind with a new duality between body/mind and spirit. I searched and am searching for a new, more integrated way of being that honors each expression as equal. As beings who contain both the body and the mind, we also contain the spiritual realm of pure consciousness, infinite peace and unconditional love. We are unique and have infinite potential for realization and growth while simultaneously living in a world of mind and matter. The journey to the center of our being can only be through the peaks and valleys of our experience in the world right here on Earth. What I experienced at the center of my body-mind was pure, powerful and deeply alive.

Visiting my parents for one brief month I felt strongly that the practice of yoga had changed me into a better person and given me a more peaceful mind. I also began to recognize that while words lead the way to sharing, there is not a language that fully captures the essence of a whole human being. Though I love the written and spoken word I am sometimes at odds with it. Our current language has been formulated by culture, history and tradition and necessarily contains assumptions of the past. If a truly new way of thinking, being and relating to ourselves is to take shape, then we need new words, diction and syntax to speak, write and express ourselves in the new world within.

Even though my teacher was thousands of miles away in Mysore I practiced every day diligently and felt his guidance. In some ways I was entering an integration period where the work of the spiritual path began to transform into my own inner wisdom. I began to embrace the notion that yoga is a daily practice through which you can begin to learn to listen to your body, respect its messages and take appropriate action when necessary. I saw that my body was in constant dialogue with the elements of the natural world, that it contained great wisdom and was always available to me. I learned that the body vibrates as a total greater than the sum of its many parts and includes every thought you think and every feeling you have. Each cell, muscle and tissue carries with it a memory far greater than your conscious mind can imagine. Past traumas that evoke fear, anxiety, anger or depression have a physical reality stored in the very tissue of your body. Old patterns are stored on the physical level with as much, if not more fervor than on the psychological level. My experience taught me that the body is a large physical memory bank that speaks volumes about a person's past, present and future. As I walked the same streets and beaches of my childhood, in the glorious sunshine of Miami, I also felt healed and free of the past. My body had changed shape and size to a new figure more suited to the level of peace that I experienced with myself.

I honestly felt as if each muscle, cell, organ and tissue in my body had the potential to maintain a distinct personality. Before yoga I lived in a twisted mixture of jarring sounds while now my body felt like a harmonious symphony. Yoga taught me how to peacefully evolve into the friendly, magical conductor of my own life.

Creating order in the sometimes cacophonous music that exists within your body directly relates to your basic approach to life. If you merely impose your desires on your body without taking the time to listen you might also impose your will on others without taking the time to listen. If you ignore the complaints that an organ constantly gives you and take pills to dull the pain you might also find yourself ignoring some of life's major messages when they delivered to you and simply hammer away toward the end result. If you jump at every little signal in your body that even remotely recalls a painful sensation and move into a treatment plan so too might you jump at the beck and call of other people's requests. If you overdramatize the sensations you receive from your body in a deep identification with your pain you might also had a tendency to lapse into melodramatic reverie.

I started listening to my body in earnestness after my first yoga class, but only really mastered the technique during my trips to India and Nepal. Being back in Miami I was reminded of the first messages I heard when I started to really listen to my body. They were often quite confusing, but over time I began to hear my body's distinct voice in its own clear and understandable language. In my case, the relationship which formed the basis of communication had been neglected and needed time to develop. I began to see that listening was a moment-to-moment choice. Each time I ignored my body I distanced myself from it whereas each time I listened a bridge was built with the potential to unify my experience. I noticed that when I was in a stressful situation I experienced a generalized feeling of unease, queasiness, headaches, sleepless nights, increased body heat, muscle soreness, over-tiredness, lack of energy, heightened sensitivity, emotionality, increased heart-rate, increased blood pressure and/or digestive malfunction. During prolonged periods of high stress, trauma or other malicious situations I even learned to live with the body's unhappiness as normal. When I began listening to my body I made a promise to heed the early warning signs of distress, disease and unhappiness and manage my life, body, mind and spirit with spiritual intelligence. Having returned home in a geographical as well as spiritual sense, I was happy and felt, perhaps for the first time, totally myself.

There is a price to be paid when early warning signals from the body are not heeded. Areas of the body that are subject to repeated self-hatred, ignorance, pain, distress, criticism, injury, or trauma can go numb over time. This numbness is a kind of death that transforms otherwise healthy, vibrant areas into sleeping, dull ones. I maintained my meditation practice while in Miami, but when I tried to feel my stomach and my inner thighs during daily meditation it was much harder to actually sense these areas than others. In some ways they were asleep.

Similarly numerous yoga postures asked me to gain access to muscles and joints in a way that I simply could not. The muscles themselves were intact but I could not initiate any type of movement in them. The lack of feeling could have been the result of injury, pain, trauma or plain old unconsciousness. Over time I began not only feeling these sleeping areas but gaining conscious control over them. Who I was changed dramatically as a result of releasing the energy that I had devoted to pain control and suppression.

Your body is perhaps your most fundamental, grounding relationship with the world. You, a spiritual being residing within your physical body, have at your disposal a powerful tool that allows you to take shape in the world. Your body is the basic unit of physical expression in which you can evaluate the level of your vibration or life force. It is a reflection of the inner state and it provides an abundance of signs and guideposts in your daily life that let you know how you are doing.

If you seem happy on the surface yet underneath there is an old habit pattern of anger, resentment or bitterness, at some level, that is what you share. You cannot fake, beg or borrow consciousness. You are what you are and your body simply cannot lie. You have experienced only what you have experienced and as such you can share only that which you are. Although you may like the idea of sharing peace and love with the world, until you are truly, deeply peaceful you will at some level create more of the same misery that lies burning underneath your skin. The real quest towards peace begins with the quiet, steadfast searching that defines life on the path of yoga. I began to feel a commitment towards sharing the practice of yoga as an authentic search for inner peace with others. I taught my Mom and Dad the meditation techniques that I learned while on the Vipassana retreat and shared Ashtanga Yoga with every one of my friends who was interested. In Miami it was an uphill battle to erect a spiritual community so my initial yearning to be an ambassador for yoga was not met easily. But after a month, this yearning from within me grew. My body and mind were speaking clearly. I left to visit Tim in Europe and there I found a more open audience for the beginning of my message.

CHAPTER SIX
HUMILITY AND STRENGTH

A heat wave hit northern Europe in the summer of 2003 and the sun shined from the tip of Spain to the archipelago islands of Finland. Even London and Copenhagen got their share of warm weather. In the smoldering atmosphere of a baked Scandinavia I met Tim again. Where a searching girl left her Danish lover in India, a woman greeted the man she had loved on a hot August day. I felt a lifetime older from when I began the process of self-realization. It was nothing like the blessed out images of saints. It was hard work, meant to be faced squarely with understanding, courage and strength. Whatever faith I had in life was now faith in the process of my evolution. Whatever belief I had in the beauty of the world was now grounded within my own direct experience.

Tim had been deeply entrenched in creating Hendrix House, a dance performance based on the life of Jimi Hendrix. Wilda, his dance company, was fully funded by the Danish government and he was an internationally known choreographer set to make his next work in Finland. Our separate worlds that we'd worked so hard to build, were set to collide.

I arrived in Europe with an invitation to teach my first yoga workshop in Galway and Dublin. This allowed me the chance to have two reasons for crossing the Atlantic Ocean. Here was a great opportunity to define myself on totally new terms in the arena of yoga and love. The clear blueness of the summer sky opened onto the vast love we shared. Through nearly daily emails and intermittent phone calls over crackling telephone lines our hearts had carved a pathway deep into each other's souls. During those calls and emails I learned of Tim's passion for dance and movement and his discovery of yoga as a healing tool. He had lived in New York City in his twenties and pursued his dream of being a dancer. When he eventually returned to Denmark in his late twenties, the Danish Cultural Ministry awarded him a grant to develop his choreographic dreams. Yoga came into his life after a bad fall from a mountaintop in Venezuela. He was twenty-five at the time and the accident nearly ended his dance career. He slipped off a dry river bed, plummeting nearly eight stories to land on his legs, breaking his left heel, both knees, right elbow, nose and right thigh bone. He was actually lucky because every other person who fell from that spot died on impact. Two years later when he had learned how to walk and dance again he joined a yoga class in New York City, focusing his attention on his knees, which had never fully recovered. By the time I met Tim he had a whole career behind him, a life where he was cherished and loved. I was impressed, inspired and intimidated.

That August day felt like magic. Every kiss was sacred and holy. Six months in separate countries had not dampened the electricity of the connection. We shared our feelings without reservation. Greedily, we basked in the feeling of being in love, drinking presence, skin and lips at every chance like two angels playing in fields of love, healing old wounds with every touch. Blinded by our own brightness we lost ourselves in the sea of our own skin. It felt like we could do anything together. So when we started to reach the end of summer it was only natural that we decided to go to Mysore together to avoid the winter. In some ways I feel like that summer was a false advertisement for summer in Northern Europe. It really did feel like the sun never stopped shining, for two months straight, but I've been to Europe every summer for the last eight years and I have never seen that much sun in Denmark since.

Throughout the summer Hendrix House grew so successful that Tim thought it might be the pinnacle of his career and began considering retiring as a dancer. He even considered, ever so briefly, the idea of leaving dance to pursue a life of yoga. But what he thought was just a passing thought proved more like a premonition. I left Tim in Europe for one month to return to Miami and we met again en route to India. Arriving in Mysore in January 2004 hand in hand, openly expressing feelings we could not contain, we walked the streets intertwined, disobeying the unspoken law of the land not to display public. It was a need beyond us that worked itself through our connection. There was an urgency to spend every moment together and a fear of losing what we had.

Tim was the first man that I really trusted with the whole truth of myself. And it wasn't an easy thing to open up completely. There were stories from my past that I had not told another living person and through his sincere wish to know me without judgment he created a space where I felt comfortable to speak openly about things that I was ashamed of. This was new territory for me. Sharing space, hearts, sex and love Tim and I explored new directions. His presence gave me a new idea of men. Sex and love, always two distinct ideas in my mind, would finally merge. Three months into our stay we were on a steady routine. Sleeping at 8 PM, rising at 3 AM, practicing at 5 AM. Our lives were in perfect synch.

On my first two trips to India my main method of transportation was my two feet and rickshaws, but now on my third trip I would be a passenger on a motorcycle. The Danish ride bicycles everywhere so Tim was familiar with life on a two-wheeler. He rented a scooter for the first week and then a friend loaned him an old black and silver British-inspired motorcycle called an Enfield. I'm no speed junkie but I must admit that the deep rumbling sound these vehicles make is sexy. Tim taught himself to drive by going slowly up and down the street in front of our apartment. At first he couldn't figure out how to brake so he just coasted. After a week he felt confident enough to have me as a passenger. With our newly found freedom, we drove the streets of Mysore together.

Mysore was now our place and yoga our shared bond together. We stayed in a brand new building the in center of Gokulam called Sri Vara Manor. By Indian standards it was a brilliant high-rise condominium with all the conveniences of modern life. For just around three hundred dollars a month we had three bedrooms, two bathrooms, three balconies, marble floors throughout and a kitchen with our own water filter. In this spacious apartment we welcomed mutual friends and Tim devoted one whole bedroom to planning his next dance piece with Wilda, his company. After three months of cooking, loving and being together, this shared space became a home for both our spiritual pursuits and our relationship. Then we dove into our yoga. Tim quickly completed the Second Series of Postures while I was working on the Third Series of Postures. And while I was already familiar with Guruji and Sharath this was Tim's first visit to Mysore and both of us quickly learned how to support each other through the emotional ups and downs that yoga practice can sometimes bring out.

While we both worked very hard and devoted most of our time to yoga, during our time off we went back to exploring Mysore. I remember particularly enjoying having to speak with locals in a broken English that they had invented. After some time, I realized it was far more effective than speaking plain English. For example, rather than "please make a right turn," I learned to say "right turning possible; ordering tea without sugar became "sugarless tea" and "how are you" transformed into "had your lunch".

We loved spending afternoons in the Devarajurs Market in Mysore, which was a call back to an old era of India's past. I remember we'd enter through a pair of granite pillars you and then be engulfed by stacks of colorful vegetables, glittering bangles, exotic fruits, pure oils, jasmine, rose garlands and pyramid shaped pigment powder. We would often be harassed into buying incense, or find ourselves listening to small children singing "Hotel California". It was the sort of market where you practiced your bargaining skills and could purchase a variety of objects such as red bananas, green eggplants, magenta face powder, "American" diamond bracelets, and sandalwood oil for just under ten dollars.

Nestled in a strip of stores that lined the entrance to this historic market, Ashok was and remains the oldest and most respected bookstore in Mysore. The owner of the store is a lover of literature in both English and his native tongue. I ventured into town nearly once a week to buy a serving of the English language and converse, at least in written word, with a grammatically correct version of my language. On one such occasion, feeling serious and introspective I returned to our apartment with a copy of the Tibetan Book of Dead.

On Tuesday night in late March Tim and I read aloud to each other from the Tibetan Book of Dead. While reading about the transmigration of the soul we felt our past and future twist together. Then, suddenly, one of Mysore's ubiquitous power cuts kicked in (which was not altogether surprising). Still, at the exact same moment an unusual wind breezed through the hallway of our apartment. Reading by candlelight the flames flickered unnaturally. We couldn't help but be caught up in the mysticism, and to this day feel that moment by candlelight truly solidified our relationship. It gave meaning to everything we had shared. We offered our prayers as the lights clicked on; a dead calm replaced the fast moving air and a neighbor's sing song radio oozed into our rooms. Life went on.

The next morning I awoke with a sense of relief. There was nothing I would take for granted in my life ever again. I was so happy just to be myself. More focused, steady and determined than I had ever been, I threw myself back into my yoga practice, my life and myself. A new fire ignited deep within me. I was determined to be strong where I was weak before. I was determined to actively, consciously and powerfully choose to create the life I wanted. I was also in the midst of a very challenging period of my studies in yoga.

I was learning the ten arm balances of Third Series from my teachers in Mysore. These are one of the great gates of the Ashtanga Yoga practice. For me they were like running the gauntlet, and my daily practice took almost three hours to fully complete. Each day I was reminded that lifting my butt off the ground in any way proved to be one of the most insurmountable movements in the entire yoga practice. After years of dedicated practice I was only a little better at it. I felt weak, unsure and unsteady.

It was so hot and sweaty at 5 AM that beads of perspiration had already accumulated on Tim's back, even before practice. The heat made me feel as if I had lost all my strength, so the notion of doing a three-hour practice where all the hardest strength postures came at the end was beyond daunting. As it was, these postures were lined up one after another with little or no break between them. I trudged through the practice and poured so much of my heart and soul into the movement that I was not sure if I was actually getting stronger or just killing myself. I asked Tim to help me with some technical and anatomical analysis since his background in dance gave him a deeply perceptive insight into the mechanics of motion, but nothing seemed to help. I nearly gave up faith that I would ever complete the Third Series at all.

One day I actually felt like I was getting stronger, but apparently I was still quite feeble. Sharath looked at me and said, "Kino, you have to be stronger." The feeling of quitting overtook me. And yet I managed to connect with Guruji's heart this gave me the faith I needed to carry on. On days when I simply had no more to give, Guruji would ask for more, telling me to "lift up". And when I tried I discovered more strength than I ever thought possible.

The first time I moved through the complete set of postures in Mysore my arms lost all connection to bone and turned instead to soft rubber. Drinking from a glass was impossible; I needed a straw. The arm balances are so called because in these postures the only thing that touches the ground is your hand. The entire weight of the body is balanced on the arms with various feet, legs and positions being taken by the torso and other limbs. To say that it's hard is simply not enough; it is impossible, beyond challenging, gymnastic and graceful. The advanced section is part of what's called Stira Baga, or strength and grace. It takes a disciplined mind and a strong body to lift, bend and move the way the advanced practice asks you to move. It is not for the weak of heart, nor the feeble in spirit. The weak bodied can learn strength, but you'll need a strong spirit to carry you through.

My experience was a mixture of intense effort and surprise. One afternoon when I was feeling doubtful about my practice I went to speak with Guruji and Sharath. Much to my shock that day I received the authorization letter stating that I could now officially teach Ashtanga Yoga. It was only my third trip to Mysore and I was humbled by the experience. But more than that, when I stood in the office holding the letter Sharath then suggested that I should take the higher level of qualification called "the certification" on my next trip. This was something I had never even conceived of. I was happy to just have the authorization.

Through it all I was filled with gratitude, all of it having opened throughout the last months' self-realization. I always wanted to find my calling, my passion—my reason for being. Finally, I had a clear-cut view of my life path. I had a message to bring to the world about strength of spirit and I would devote myself tirelessly to sharing that with others. I felt like the laws of spirit spoke to me and gave me a mission to help people believe in themselves and develop the tenacity it takes to see their dreams all the way through to completion, no matter how long it might take. My normally bouncing mind was directed, calm and focused.

Looking back I see how difficult it was for me to get to this point and how hard it was for me to let go of my past. Life learning happens at exactly the pace with which you are willing to let go of ways of being that no longer serve your spiritual growth. When you are truly ready to learn you can cross milestones in minutes. As difficult as the arm balances were to take on I understood that postures did not come from forcing my body to do things it did not want to do, but instead from listening to my body's wisdom.

Strength is actually softness; through yoga I learned that I needed to be strong in a way that bends and gives while maintaining a foundation. I began to learn that this balance was a masterful feat of body and mind unity. Strength without a compassionate connection to the tender heart of love is not strength at all. Instead true strength is a balanced mix of understanding and the ability to go above and beyond. True strength actually has no limit or end and does not require that you waste energy creating it. Instead the strength that we all really need is within. It sits at the center of our being, fueled by the limitless power of love.

After exhausting myself beyond what I ever thought possible in the road to achieving challenging arm balances and inversions I finally let go of the disbelief and effort. This letting go was a surrender that opened my mind to a deeper level of strength. At the beginning of May after spending five months in India together, Tim returned to Europe to begin choreographing his next dance performance and I spent the last month of my stay in India by myself. When the time was over I left Mysore to meet Tim in Europe where I would spend the next six months together with him. Far from just a visit, I was now filled with a passion to share my experience of inner strength with others. Before I left India I would go for one last coconut, one last chai and say goodbye to my teachers. As I sat in the office with both Guruji and Sharath I offered myself to them again and asked, "What is it that you would like me to focus on in my practice?" Guruji said, "You doing advanced practice, good." I smiled, but before I could enjoy that moment Sharath looked at me and said, "Still weak, strength not coming, still a little wobbly." Rather than fall apart or collapse into self-pity or doubt I just watched my emotions play before me like a movie. Once I regained my center I said, "Thank you" to both of my teachers and touched Guruji's feet once more before the taxi to Bangalore airport picked me up. During the fourteen-hour journey back to Denmark I was filled with a strength and determination that I had never known before.

There is a power source in the center of every human being that only gets stronger when pressed. This expansive energy generator is love. When you go deeper into it, this real strength only gets stronger. On a physical level there is a solid structural foundation that translates into effortless strength. This structural integration means that no, one body part is acting without total connection to the whole. The arms are not strong by themselves, nor the stomach, legs or back. Instead this interconnected way of moving and being means that the whole body is strong together. The process of being strong in yoga is more about finding that sweet spot of harmonic balance than building muscle.

Strength is a state of mind that is practiced in every arm balance and inversion. Living in Mysore with Tim, completing the arm balances in Third Series and learning the lesson of strength was what defined my 2004 trip to India. During this third trip to India a passion to share these lessons became my life's mission. I gained a new awareness about the method of yoga postures to teach life lessons. Every moment of your yoga practice cultivates the kind of spiritual endurance that you need to meet life with peace of mind in even the most stressful situations. There is perhaps nothing more ugly than lashing out at friends and loved ones simply because you are feeling overwhelmed. A beautiful person has the steady mind of a peaceful yogi. Strength is a decision you make about your ability to stay with a problem until you find the answer. When everything inside of you wants to quit, break down and fall apart there is a small voice of resounding courage in your heart ready to give it another try. True strength also bends when bending is hard. It is by knowing intimately the depths of power within that you will experience lasting peace.

And then, with strength, comes love. Everyone is familiar with love. I myself spent many years grappling with its meaning in my life, and like so many I learned that there is nothing stronger than it. First I learned to love my teacher, Guruji, whose presence gave me faith, devotion and dedication. Then I fell in love with Tim who taught me how to share love. Finally I fell in love with myself when I began to believe in my own inner strength. Love is the connective tissue of the human race and challenging yoga postures can teach you how to soften into the feeling of love as an expression of inner strength. Yoga teaches you how to have faith in the things that you do not see and it is through the endless power of love that yoga transforms practitioners. It certainly did in my case.

Human beings have this amazing capacity to love, open their hearts and be with each other in a deep and meaningful way. The smallest word or tone of voice can break or open a friend's heart. We are tender creatures, full of love. With the same fervor that we love, our hearts also break. Yoga demands that we keep our faith in moments of distress, injury or pain so that when we experience difficult moments in our life we are able to remain calm and peaceful. I was tested both in my life and in my yoga practice, and in both instances I found strength beyond anything I imagined possible. I took this strength, particularly that which I had gained in Mysore and carried it into the world as a teacher.

Once you find that minimal amount of strength required to perform arm balances and inversions and you can lift yourself up in manners that once seemed impossible. You become filled with a shining glow of confidence. When you use yoga postures to explore places in your body and your mind where you have never been before you gain access to the very place in your being that will carry you through difficult times.

Yoga demands that strength comes from inter connectedness of the body and mind so that in life you never act from a false sense of hubris. In your body you are only as strong as the overall integration of unity. If you expect your arms to lift you while acting in a vacuum, divorced from your body, you will fail. But if you learn to integrate your arms with the solid structural foundation of every joint, tissue, organ and bone in your body then you will have access to the limitless strength within. With daily spiritual practice yoga practitioners learn to be more authentic in their relationships. They learn how to listen to themselves and others and maintain the openhearted wisdom that friendship and family life demands.

As an only child, relationships have always been one of my greatest tests. I always thought I was better off alone. But just as the body in yoga is only strong when in union, we are only strong when we mesh together and act as one.

Spending five months in India with Tim helped me experience how true intimacy adds value and meaning to life. As I looked ahead to the next six months that we would share in Europe for the summer and fall I was both excited and nervous. Our India was a storybook romance but the reality of sharing and creating a life together in our home countries loomed over us as a great challenge. I remember first being told that learning to live in harmonious balance was a necessary step along the journey of yoga. I learned this the hard way and yet it's such a simple lesson. By developing the strength to accept yourself where you are while simultaneously demanding that you do more means that you have made peace with your journey.

For most of us it takes great strength to ask life's difficult questions and remain open to the answers, for the answers themselves are only a beginning and not always the ones we expect. We sometimes find ourselves in the midst of great turbulence in our lives or at a perplexing intersection of past, present and future. In order to cultivate the kind of mind that quietly and calmly faces life's challenges, you must practice regularly at developing your strength. Realize that when you come into contact with people in the midst of inner turmoil, you might not notice their quiet strength. You might not have noticed your own while you were in a similar space. Rest assured that a steady, calm place of strength exists in you, in me...in each of us. And it is in the most questioning moments of our life when we can access the inner stores of power. It is not during easy moments that you will find yourself practicing steady strength but instead during moments when you feel the greatest insecurity. It is in these moments that you are growing stronger. Know that the turbulent sea creates in your core a depth that will never leave you.

Part of my path in yoga has been to find out just how far I was willing to go in order to achieve the results I want—to find strength and love. In the first years of practicing yoga I tried to beat my body into being strong and yet I knew no strength. Instead I got injured, felt dry and this perpetuated a rejection of my female softness. Over time I learned to love my weaknesses as essential components of strength and as keys to the inter connectedness of humanity. While it would have been easy to just quit and say that the more challenging yoga postures or life challenges were too difficult for me, I searched for a true source of power. I could have said that Ashtanga Yoga was too radical, too severe, too rigid but instead I found a peace within the challenges of my daily discipline.

My teacher's words and his unshakable presence gave me the courage to continue practicing even when it felt impossible. I made sacrifices and made the commitment to see my yoga journey through to the end. And ultimately, my searching led me to the life experiences that helped me see myself completely.

CHAPTER SEVEN
THE BIRTH OF A TEACHER

When Tim and I left Mysore we agreed to live in Europe for about six months together starting in June 2004. He was working on one of the last big projects of his acclaimed dance company Wilda. I was launching my website. The internet was opening doors that simply did not exist before and I was in awe of the level of connectivity that could reach across nationalities, borders, geographies, and time zones. Within one month of my website's release I had a dozen workshops booked throughout Europe and North America. The initial days of teaching were like the slow steady path towards strength in the yoga practice. Whereas before I had taught classes and workshops for very few people in Miami, now the number of people in my classes and workshops increased, eventually swelling to large numbers. I worked hard at it from the beginning, just as I had worked at my physical yoga practice.

I was particularly astounded that my gender seemed to be opening doors for me. In a relative dearth of female accomplished Ashtanga Yoga teachers, my website and teaching seemed to be interesting and perhaps inspiring too. Female practitioners who found it hard to relate to male teachers could easily relate with my personal experience. When I spoke of strength, women listened intently and personally. The more I taught the more I wanted to wholly dedicate myself to teaching others what I had learned, sharing the fruits of my labor. The beauty that other people always said they saw in me now truly flowered, blossomed and bloomed. A new strength began to grow within me and I found stores of endurance, poise and grace I did not know I had.

Within a very short time my life consisted of guest teaching weekend yoga workshops, leading yoga retreats and teaching classes all over the world. The airport was and is still one of my most familiar sights. In August of the 2004 I visited four different European cities teaching Ashtanga Yoga. The nestled mountain city of Zurich greeted me with twenty students, Copenhagen's old world coziness brought thirty and Frankfurt's festival weekend turned out more than forty. Throughout all of this traveling that summer in Northern Europe, one thing did strike me—how cold it was! I had no concept of a summer without sunshine, but apparently the Danish did.

I remember there was a warm, sunny day in May and then it became rainy and grey, and stayed that way for three months straight. Whenever I mentioned it to people they shrugged, "Oh, yeah, a bad summer." And although my teaching was thriving, being from the land of eternal summer where the weather is hot and hotter, with chance of sun and partial sun, this "bad" summer nearly killed me. I was seasonally depressed from a lack of sunshine and generally in a bad mood about having to run the heating in August. Tim had his work to distract him and he spent most days locked behind the mirrored walls of a dance studio. I sat in a country whose language and culture were more foreign to me than India. Things got even worse in September when I traveled to Ireland. While I fell in love with the beauty of this country, let's face it, it's not exactly tropical. I remember they had the heating on for the first weekend of September.

When Tim's dance project was finished at the end of September he was less than satisfied. Teetering on the edge of changing his career he decided to experiment with teaching yoga alongside me while traveling through the U.S. Since Tim was on a break between dance pieces and I wanted to visit my family in Miami, the timing couldn't be better. We taught yoga workshops at centers in Boston, New York and Charlottesville. Then Tim and I returned to Mysore in for January through March 2005 for two quick months and completed the Third Series. After that I was no longer hungry for a sense of achievement and my direction shifted outward into defining my life's purpose. I was scheduled to teach more than ever, with at least two workshops each month throughout the summer in Europe. Tim was set to put on yet another dance performance, this one inspired by the life of Hans Christen Andersen. When the piece was finished he again felt less than satisfied—the performance got mixed reviews—and he wondered whether he had made a mistake to not let it all go. As I pondered another five months in Europe I was already fearful of the weather.

Suddenly it was September and I was back in Ireland for a second visit. The workshop was in a new studio and there were many more students. That was the good part and I was grateful for it. Then on the night before my first class after a day of viewing the sights of Dublin Castle and shopping on Pearse Street from under a wind-torn umbrella, I found myself in a cold bathroom wondering how to get warm. I sat at the edge of a bathtub filling the ceramic casing with boiling water to thaw out my freezing joints. Suddenly an image of turquoise water glistened in my memory and I felt a calling. Not for vacation, but for a return to the sunshine that is my home. On a cold night a few weeks prior to this momentary realization I dreamt of leaping into a warm sea with the sun beating down on my face, my body and my thighs. I wanted to go back to Miami. Not only did I just want to go back to the warm beaches of my youth, but I wanted also to create a center for yoga there. A dream was born.

I was reluctant to share my dream with Tim because it meant he would probably have to give up his established life and career in Denmark. Although he was interested in a break from his dance it was hard to give up something he devoted so much of his life to. Dancers from all over Europe respected Tim's company and his vision for movement. He was a star in the dance world and it would be a lot to let go of. But the timing was right so Tim took the plunge and gave it a try.

We returned to Miami for November, taught in Mexico, Boston, New York City and Tampa together and started searching for commercial spaces suitable for a yoga center. We searched all around Miami and then found the perfect space on South Beach owned by a Bangladeshi man who made us feel like we never left India. We signed a five-year lease, established a corporation called Miami Life Center and began construction of a yoga center on Miami Beach.

Naively we planed a trip to India for January and February of 2006, just when our lease started. We had no idea what we were getting in to, but we did know that we were in it together. Thinking the permits would easily pass through the city's planning department and construction would be completed when we returned, we trusted our builders to get the job done. Bad move. From the time we signed the lease to the date we officially opened our doors was a full nine months and far more money than we initially planned on. In September, after a long and tortuous round through Miami Beach permitting departments, one construction meltdown after another and more stress than I have ever experienced, we welcomed our first yoga students into Miami Life Centre.

Iced ruby travertine floors were laid in large tiles ready to greet the soles of bare yogis feet. A limestone wall housed a planter with Floridian ferns, green and variegated varieties. A nearly three foot tall Buddha statue holding the gesture of openness sat at the center of the lobby's shrine. Two oversized comfy red supplex couches padded the bottoms of hard-worked yoga practitioners. After all this time, all this devotion to yoga and finding myself, after all my trips to Mysore, Nepal, Europe and now a new teaching career that was sending me all over the world—in the end what I wanted was very simple, and I wanted it back in the sunny, sandy place by sea I knew as home. I was eager to trade a cold bathroom in northern Europe for a sunny winter day in the south. My loving partner, Tim was eager to spend his life with me and together we started a new life in Miami.

The sunshine flooded every sunset with ethereal lights, hues and clouds. Wet, humid warmth greeted the yoga students who entered this new space. Bamboo floors, photos of Guruji and Sharath, a blessed space complete with showers, changing rooms and two studios for yoga, holistic health and consciousness. The journey into the world of yoga created a forum for my spiritual development. In a public offering to the people of Miami I worked together with Tim, my future husband, and Greg Nardi, my dear friend, to create a home for true spiritual practice in heart of Miami Beach.

We opened Miami Life Centre in 2006 and in January 2007 Tim and I planned another trip to Mysore together. I was twenty-nine on this sixth trip to Mysore. Tim and I were committed to each other and to the journey of teaching yoga together. He still had his dance company and would do a few more pieces, but we were building the foundation of our shared life together.

Then one day Tim presented me with a bouquet of roses, got down on one knee and asked me to marry him. We had the whole trip in Mysore together to ponder the idea of living permanently in the U.S. and creating a life together based on a shared dream of yoga. Things couldn't be better.

We progressed deeper into the practice, though I was always afraid of starting the Fourth Series. It made no sense to me and I heard horror stories of people who injured themselves or were injured by the help of a teacher. I wanted to stay away from it. But on this trip I was given the first two postures of this even more challenging series. The best part of this trip had nothing to do with postures.

It was a Sunday in February and I found myself in the front of a large room ten times the size of the old shala with nearly 300 people vying for a position near Guruji's feet. I remember my first trip to Mysore and how my question to Guruji had changed the course of my life. Now I had another question. With humility, reverence and respect in my voice, I asked my teacher another question, "Guruji, on my first trip to Mysore, I asked you how I could find inner peace. Your answer gave me inspiration and faith to practice all these years. Now I am teaching this yoga as you have taught me, what can I say to new students to give them that same gift you gave to me?"

The presence of so many more people practicing Ashtanga Yoga is something that Guruji always loved to see. Guruji leaned in to catch my gaze. Then he paused, smiled, perhaps remembering our previous conversation nearly five years before and said, in his whimsical broken English, "You tell them same."

Again it was something indescribable that touched me deeply, something beyond the words. Perhaps it was in the silence that struck before the words were spoken. Guruji was a man with few English words, a wide-open heart, and years of dedication to a yoga practice. He was a man with great strength, wisdom and temper.

A simple method: posture, breathing and gaze. One teacher, one style of yoga, many, many years of practice and then peace will certainly come. Guruji used to say, "Ashtanga yoga is for all people... old people, young people, fat people, skinny people...only not lazy people." That is because Ashtanga yoga is challenging; it asks tightness to bend, softness to be strong and pushes the limits of the mind and the body beyond popular medical notions of safety and comfort. In doing so practitioners literally expand their consciousness.

On that same trip Tim received the Authorization to teach Ashtanga Yoga and I received the prestigious and rare Certification to teach Ashtanga yoga from Guruji. In North America, I have since learned, there are less than twenty people who hold this title and I am the youngest person and the youngest woman to receive this blessing. It was an understatement to say I was very proud of this achievement, and yet it also meant that there was nothing left to fight for. Instead of waging war, I could create a dream out of the purity of the dream itself. The vibrancy of life was free to express itself however it liked in me.

* * *

At the end of each week in the New Shala everyone does a Guided Primary Series together. Tim and I had just taken Guruji's class. It was the last time I would see Guruji before he got sick and his level of teaching changed. After practice we lined up to pay our respects and do pranam with our teacher. When I laid my hands on his feet once more and looked up at him, Guruji smiled his innocent yet knowing smile and said, "Your letter, it's ready." Then he directed me with towards his desk but realized that he hadn't signed it yet. So he said, "You wait." There were still thirty students who were waiting in a line to say thanks to Guruji. After all were done we sat down and filled out my Certification letter.

I watched nervously in disbelief, my heart tied to his every move. There were old stamps kept in a raggedy box with official caliber from the government of India. He took each one out and placed his stamp of approval on the form. After signing his name he handed the form to me, smiling ear to ear. I thanked him again and he hugged me. I was so excited I felt like I was floating and rushed outside to show Tim. We would return to Miami with new qualifications for our center and with the true and highest blessing of our teacher.

While in some ways this was the end I couldn't help but feel it was just the beginning. Now I would dedicate my life to sharing the tradition of Ashtanga Yoga with as many people as possible in the small hope that I could continue the dream of my teacher to bring yoga to the world.

CHAPTER EIGHT
SEE ALL THE WAY THROUGH

During the summer of 2007 Tim and I visited Europe to spend time with his family in Denmark and I also joined my third Vipassana Meditation Course in August, this time in Belgium. After almost a year in business in Miami I needed a break, and was looking forward to taking some time to reflect and return to my centre. After a long arduous journey on Belgian buses I found myself in the beautiful mid-European countryside during a heat wave. Miami is fully equipped for heat but Belgium, not so much.

The meditation retreat was built to protect students from the cold, not relieve them from sweltering heat. It was set in an idyllic field of trees that any other time would have been ideal, but this summer was a scorcher. The brown mulch had steam rising from the ground and the only breeze brought hot air. What an irony for me to actually want the cold after moving to Miami and yet receive more heat! Never have I prayed for cold weather so much. I came to sit and explore the inner terrain within myself and all I felt and focused on for eight days was the unforgiving heat. Desperate for relief I fantasized about jumping into a cool pool of water as a break from the rigorous meditation practice schedule. It was even hot at 4 AM, hotter than India's humid dampness. It was dry, crackling heat like an oven that smolders and roasts you from the inside like a karmic fire.

It is no surprise that heat is a symbol of anger and I felt like I was sitting in a fiery pool of emotion for eight days. I sat there, hot, miserable and annoyed trying to make peace with the experience. Then one day while I was lying in my room during a break I had a kind of vision or daydream of sorts–it's hard to explain, exactly. I saw my eyes in the body of another woman living in another era. She was a nun and was on her knees praying before the altar in a church. What was unique about her was the prayer she repeated. With desperation she clasped her hands together and prayed to be able to perform the priest's duties. She was angry at the way the nuns were treated and wanted the freedom afforded to men. The anger ran deep and was directed at the church, at the men who ran the church and even towards the Christian concept of God. I was never one to have "visions" of things from the future or past but yoga opened my mind so that when this experience happened I was able to embrace it and follow it. This was something that I saw and felt with my eyes closed and I couldn't explain or just dismiss it. The "dream" then flashed forward to a priest ten years later, but with the nuns face, and she was walking through a small town in the French countryside. The church was short of priests and allowed her to live out her dream if she was willing to hide her femininity. She did so but ultimately died a martyr unable to make peace with herself, men or the church. I opened my eyes.

I was shocked to find I had anger towards men that had been lurking inside of me for a really long time. Up until that pivotal moment I had no idea I was carrying any sort of antagonism toward anyone. This came as a humbling epiphany to see that I was harboring such a giant, negative emotion inside of myself. Suddenly I realized that I was motivated not always out of selfless service or pure intention, but instead by conflict at a very deep level.

As I looked back at my past relationships I realized that they were not always born of a true seed of shared love. There were situations where I had been the victim and others that left a scar in my heart too deep for me to face up to until this moment. Drawing a line from my first romantic interlude as a young teenager to the present, one key thread was prevalent throughout—a feeling of antagonism. Slowly I began to see how I was never able to be with a person whom I loved in a mutual state of support, ease and flow. It seemed as if my early, unsuccessful relationships had warped my sense of what a relationship should be and how men could and would behave and, as a result, I had wandered through my adult life fighting with the opposite sex. Even in the field of yoga where I devoted my life to peace and self-love, I inadvertently fought the predominately male instructors who guided me.

The more I analyzed these feelings the more they made sense. When I compared myself with naturally strong men in the Ashtanga Yoga practice I had always felt uncomfortable. In a sense I was driven to prove that a woman could do anything, if not more, than a man could and this, in turn, created negative feelings towards men. I could see now that my motivation was not, by any means, pure. Instead it was based in a very old pattern of reaction. If I was going to truly carry the message of Ashtanga Yoga to the world and be an inspirational figure for women (and men too), then I would need to work through this deep-seated anger.

For two years prior to this fateful moment I had a burning sensation in my left sacra-iliac joint every time I tried to do deep backbends in my yoga practice. I didn't think much as to why I suffered this sensation but tried every form of treatment and therapy possible. Nothing worked. The moment I saw this vision memory the pain intensified to a degree that I had not experienced before. Yoga believes in the connection of the body and mind. The emotional body stores memories and experiences that can transcend the physical life form. I began to understand that the pain I had been suffering in my yoga practice was directly related to this deeply held anger. And it did not vanish in one fell swoop of liberation, though that would have been nice.

Around this time I truly began to understand that the only reason yoga asks practitioners to attempt increasingly hard postures is because it takes tying the body in a knot to wake up all the tissues, joints and parts of the sleeping self. This newfound pain led me on a journey of self-discovery that forced me to confront a vicious anger that I had no idea was inside. Until I was fully conscious of the unconscious thought patterns running in my mind there was no way I could gain any control over them.

I started addressing this anger and pain by using one of the basic teachings of yoga: breathe into your pain. The magic of the breath both calms the mind and turns your attention away from the troubling circumstance at hand. Sometimes a moment of pause is all that is needed to find the strength to choose a new way of being. Yoga transforms the body not by substituting one experience for another, but instead by teaching practitioners how to stay in difficult situations without running away.

I also began to embrace the constant of change. Both Ashtanga Yoga and Vipassana meditation share the notion that spiritual practice strengthens the mind so that when you experience the inevitable ups and downs of life you are no longer deeply disturbed by them. The only thing that you can really count on is that things will inevitably change. What feels good will one day feel bad and vice versa. The good part about this is when you feel strong negative emotions you can rest assured that they will one day pass away. The type of higher mind cultivated by years of dedicated practice is a strong mind that can sense, feel and acknowledge the stickiest emotions without fueling the fire. No matter how intense or stuck we may feel in our emotions, sooner or later they will change. After all, anger cannot create peace. Itching the scab that started the whole conflagration will not end it. Trying to "get" a new posture that you cannot easily understand while lost in a state of anger is a waste of time. The middle way that yoga teaches is a better solution—with the cool, calm light of observation, you are able to create a space of transformation in your practice and in your life. Rather than reacting by running from unhappy moments, the basic teaching of spiritual practice is to find yourself in the midst of your greatest challenge and manage to stay with it, observe it rather than react to it out of habit. For example, when you find yourself in the throws of anger with heat rising up your spine, blood boiling and eyes narrowing, the normal reaction is to let it spew out from your mouth and body in a rising torment that attacks all beings around. But if you begin to understand that you are not your emotions and that your powerful presence is larger than any sensation that arises, you might begin to tap into a whole new way of relating to yourself and others. The Yoga Sutras say that no violence is possible to a yoga practitioner who is firmly established in nonviolence. With dedication and devotion along the path of yoga we can all experience the kind of depth and powerful peace that lies at the heart of every person.

Towards the end of my retreat I began to see that rather than creating or acting out my anger I could, instead, act out of love. This state actively gives, creates, heals and inspires. It is not anger that reaches out to others in their time of need. It is not anger, nor depression, nor fear that forgives, creates new bonds and heals. It is only love that has boundless power to reach beyond the limitations of petty emotions into a new way of being. It is love which begets a more peaceful state of mind in the midst of our most trying times. Anger, depression and fear are all reactionary and restrictive, whereas love is proactive, works with the present moment and is inclusive. I felt that I had to get to a point in my life and my yoga practice where my desire for more would decrease. And with a little work, it did.

* * *

It rained for the last two days of the retreat and I had never been so happy to see a grey sky before. The oppressive heat lifted and a cool air graced the grounds. As I emerged from the last afternoon meditation on the tenth day of the retreat the sky cleared in one fast, sweeping motion to reveal a full double rainbow. The delicate prairie landscape of Belgium was flat so I could literally see where the rainbow began on the horizon. I admired the blue skies with rain falling in the distance and an amber glowing sunset fanning outwards. After nearly a week of petulant heat and two days of grey skies the double rainbow seemed like an alternative reality, one more like an acid trip than the closing of a meditation session. I sat on the concrete steps that formed the entryway to the women's dormitory and became engrossed in the sight unfolding before me. Birds chirped in the distance, the wind gently kissed my cheeks and the rainbow slowly moved across the panoramic sky. Starting its trajectory in an open field it inched forward until the colors enveloped a country house in red, orange, yellow, green, blue and violet light. If there is ever a chance to find a lepricon with a pot of gold at the end of the rainbow, this was it.

In the yoga tradition there is an idea called the body of light, where you merge so completely with divine consciousness that your body literally turns into the rainbow light of pure spirit. In the Tibetan tradition rainbows are taken as signs of spiritual realization. As I sat there that afternoon I began to truly believe that my dharma in this life was to take the message of my spiritual path and share it with the world. When I left Belgium I was free and felt that I could live my life honestly, truly and purely. You see I realized that if I was going to carry the torch of Ashtanga Yoga in the world I needed to break free from all limitations that would hinder the purity of the message—including my anger towards men. This last knot to untie during the Vipassana retreat crystallized and focused the lessons that I learned about strength. It allowed me see strength as an expression of love rather than brute force and it allowed me to life my life from a place of resolution and freedom from the past.

The battle in yoga, if there is one, is actually fought on the inner terrain. The great paradox that many long-term practitioners learn is that they are really fighting with themselves. Yoga asks us to make peace with the deepest, most secretive, terrifying and even shameful parts of ourselves. In doing we find the only way possible to make that kind of peace is by reaching to the external world as well. It is not that you will never feel irritated, frustrated, angry, sad or fearful again, but that you will learn how to manage these difficult emotions when they do arise. In actively choosing your course of action you will transform the old habituated patterns of war and fighting into peace and friendship. By doing so on the internal level you will naturally change your outer world as well. Yoga means to unify, to yoke, to bring together and one of the most omnipresent things that yoga brings together is the unity of the inner and outer worlds. Peace is a moment-to-moment choice just like healing. It is a fragile balance that is easily lost in a hateful argument. Peace is an active choice made each time we maintain our balanced mind amidst difficult circumstances. The peace of ahimsa is not boring, just as the meditator's mind is not dull. Instead this peace, like love, is a dynamic balance where life happens.

* * *

After I left the Vipassana meditation retreat in Belgium I spent a few days in Denmark and then returned to Miami. It was September and I was eager to leave behind the intensity of the retreat for the sunshine and blue skies of Florida, I felt free to create my life with openhearted faith in myself and the spiritual path. I started to feel as though I was a living testimony to the efficacy of yoga as a lifelong commitment to inner peace. I began my journey as a scared little girl and along the way discovered a beauty and strength far deeper than I ever imagined possible.

Soon after my return to Miami, in the Fall of 2007 and the Winter of 2008 Tim and I planned our wedding. We decided on the historic villa called the Charles Deering Estate. This old home is a fifteen-minute walk from the house where I grew up, along the Atlantic coast on the borders of South Miami. Tim and I are both deeply spiritual people but not affiliated with one religion or another so we chose to ask our close friend who is also an astrologer and tarot master to create a ceremony for us. While it might have been the most appropriate to ask Guruji to marry us we could not really bring him over to Miami on our budget We opted for a civil ceremony in Miami Beach city hall and a spiritually oriented ceremony by the beach. Derek Seagrieff, the astrologer who performed our wedding ceremony, organized the guests into the four elements (earth, air, fire and water) and had all parties present their embodiment of the elements and send us a blessing. Our bridesmaids and groomsmen also had to carry symbols of earth, air, fire and water to complete the ceremony. Needless to say, it was a magical, healing day.

I felt like a chapter was ending and a new one was beginning. Rather than remain focused on the deep internal work of personal practice I wanted to share the power of yoga in the world. At the Miami Life Centre Tim and I wanted to create a place for the authentic tradition of Ashtanga Yoga. We wanted to offer a true refuge for people who were pursuing a spiritual path.

When my husband and I were creating our yoga and holistic living center on Miami Beach we were filled with the initial moment of creation where great energy, passion and enthusiasm were abundant. We were wide-eyed, naive and hopeful. Then, in the nitty gritty details of bringing our dreams to fruition in the material world, we faced odds that sometimes seemed insurmountable. I remember feeling so frustrated that I wanted to quit and give up. I lost my cool more times than I care to remember. But it was my work in yoga that gave me the strength to keep going when it felt like hell. We worked every day to maintain and stay connected with the excitement of the initial moment. I realized that the larger the project I wished to undertake, the larger my tolerance for "failure" must be. In order to succeed at actualizing my dreams in the world I had to be willing to put it all on the line and be prepared to fail. In the moments when I felt miserable my steadfastness was tested and I called upon the lessons learned in my yoga practice to carry me through. Just as in yoga life presented me with situations that were beyond my natural range of ability. Yoga taught me to believe against all odds that what is impossible can truly become possible. So I applied this strong faith and determination that yoga allowed me to tap into and stayed with my dream unwaveringly until it grew into being.

At Miami Life Centre there was a steady flow of new students and new energy but rather than focus all my attention on daily classes in Miami I began teaching more traveling workshops. The more I taught the more invitations I got to teach until I actually did not have space to say yes to everyone who invited me even if I planned one to two years ahead. I was truly devoted to sharing the inspirational and healing power of yoga with as many people as possible. I released my first yoga DVD title A Journey, A Workshop and made plans to film a second, Ashtanga Yoga Primary Series. My motivation to work came from the open hearts of students in my classes both in Miami and quite literally all over the world. With the freedom to create out of a clear, unhindered space my work became pure joy. I grew committed and focused on sharing the message of yoga in more creative, innovative and forward thinking formats.

It's funny, when I was in my early twenties, when all of this began, I thought of myself as a solo butterfly with wings that would only ever be my own. In some ways I will always be the sort of person who follows the truth in their heart, but now that truth carries a much deeper message than simple pleasure. Yoga for me has always meant a total lifestyle commitment to inner peace. By choosing a partner who is also committed to the principles of yoga has helped me create a foundation of happiness. Without Tim I would be lost in the world, with only drive and focus to fulfill my life's work. I fell in love with his quirky sense of humor, honest sense of justice and valiant heart. Being with him has helped me heal the wounds of the past and given me a solid foundation to move forward. The new version of me is a woman who believes in her innate potential to achieve anything she sets her mind to. But again, things did not change on a dime, in fact, more the opposite. My journey took years of dedicated practice, patience and devotion.

Not too long ago, I found myself sitting at the uber-posh Setai hotel on Miami Beach for a brunch buffet. I was surrounded with foods from all over the world, including vegetarian options such as cinnamon apples, blueberry pancake balls, raisin waffles, fresh orange and grapefruit juice, lychee smoothies and more. The clear water of the hotel's many decorative ponds glimmered like diamonds under the Florida sun. A woman who had recently visited Miami Life Centre, my yoga centre on South Beach, was shocked to find someone she said was so "young, stylish and fabulous" the owner of such a grounded, peaceful refuge for spirituality. I was deeply flattered. She explained that she had assumed the owner of Miami Life Centre to be a much older, seasoned spiritual teacher who would fit the pre-conceived role she held in her mind for yoga master. Not that I was or am a yoga master, but she certainly felt that Miami Life Centre carried a certain gravity that she assumed only someone at a very high level of realization could found. I thanked the woman for the compliment, feeling proud that my husband and I could create something so powerful together. I leaned back in my seat, admiring the miles of sandy beach with gentle waves cresting along the shoreline and, for the first time in a long time, I felt grounded, calm, centered. A warm breeze swept my hair back and I took in a deep and thoughtful breath. I smiled then, realizing at long last that I was, truly, utterly happy.

CHAPTER NINE
TENDING THE SACRED FIRE

Yoga teaches that there is nothing to aspire to that is not already contained somewhere within us now; it is a process of discovery as much as anything else. Through practice we begin to recognize how much more powerful we are and just how connected we can be to every living thing. Yoga requires practice and study as well as the ability to be open to an entirely new paradigm of learning. Yoga requires a spiritual awakening, it requires us to push away from the nostalgic clinging to the past and become more pragmatic in our perception of how to "be" in the world. It is, in essence, a dawning of the inner light, a unique awareness of consciousness. This spiritual fire burns through obstacles and blockages that hinder the growth of true wisdom. Yoga teaches us to listen to our own inner voice. Through pain, pleasure, injury, ecstasy and bliss yoga invites practitioners to travel down the rabbit hole of personal discovery so that they may find their wonderland within.

Feeling the inner body deeply allows yoga practitioners a daily window into their own soul. By regularly "tuning in", yogis can actually feel the alignment or misalignment of their actions. The body's wisdom lies in its pervasive truthfulness and the yogi's wisdom lies in the ability to listen to the body's sometimes superior sense of self. Yoga postures or asanas give practitioners a chance to access the spiritual through the physical. This long, arduous task of internal awakening makes it possible for dedicated practitioners to excavate layers of themselves. Yogis cross the bridge between the physical and the spiritual through a path interlaced with the fire of pain, the release of trust and the free flow of love. Each physical posture presents a series of tests and challenges that heal the body and train the mind. In taking on these poses yogis gain access to a more deeply tuned-in way of living, being and acting. It is in this undulating state where the flow of life actually begins. Only with a few drops of grace can the journey reveal the inner lotus blossom at the heart of every sentient being.

Yoga is a sanctuary where we learn to listen to our body. With regular practice we can begin to actually hear the body and the mind. When our capacity to listen is at its greatest and most refined we have the ability to listen directly to our soul and seek its constant guidance. At the depths of our being lies a place where we already know all the answers to our deepest questions, a state of being so serene it remains calm even amidst the most terrifying traumas of our life.

On daily basis it is often hard to hear the musings of the subtle language of soul, with regular yoga practice it is possible to attune your sensory perception to follow the messages surfacing from the deep. The miracle of yoga is that it provides regular people like you and me a way to literally gain access to the sacred inner world of spirit. In my experience, without this check-in I would often, quite literally, be lost. I do not get the message right every time and certainly there are moments when I think I am receiving a deep message only to find that I am just feeding an old negative behavior, yoga helps me get better at listening to, trusting and having faith in the soft, but persistent voice within. Of course I didn't learn to listen on my own—like everyone else, I had a very good teacher.

* * *

Nearly ten years after the beginning of my journey into Ashtanga yoga, I found myself in the front of a large room ten times the size of the old shala with nearly three hundred people vying for a position near Guruji's feet at the weekly conference. It was January 2008 and the only thing missing was Guruji. He had taken a step back from teaching after a near-fatal infection. Sitting in the room that I knew so well with countless new students, friends and colleagues we listened to Sharath tell us that Guruji was too weak for conference.

I missed him. Guruji was a man with few English words, a wide-open heart, and years of dedication to a yoga practice. As simple as he could be, Guruji was tremendously profound. After every practice with him, I felt, suddenly, that I had changed. The same inexperienced, ignorant, naive and selfish girl did not stand in the New Shala any longer. A woman having gone through the transformation bequeathed by dedication to yoga met her teacher as a teacher herself. I realized that the way to inner realization was much more straightforward than I had always perceived it. There was and remains a simple method: posture, breathing and focus—one teacher, one style of yoga, many many years of practice.

On this Seventh visit to Mysore I had come to see my ailing teacher and pay my respects. The New Shala, not so new anymore, was now called the Shala by current yoga students. Mysore joined the technological revolution. Wi-Fi was everywhere and internet cafes that catered to the Western yoga crowd multiplied like a new fast food chain. An airport was being planned for Mysore and Starbuck's tried to vie for a position in the local coffee industry.

My Guru, Sri K. Pattabhi Jois, the man whom everyone was coming to study with, had certainly put in his years of practice. He dedicated over sixty-five years to teaching, the first thirty living in relative poverty. In the 1970s there were around five students at the Old Shala in Lakshmipuram and yet Guruji didn't quit or give up on the teaching. In the 1980s there were around forty students. In the 1990s he began reaching one hundred. Every yoga student who felt some benefit from their practice owed a debt to Pattabhi Jois, not a monetary debt, but a karmic debt of the soul. If it were not for his years of selfless service and dedication, we would not have this practice today.

I quickly realized that everything I was I owed to Guruji and Sharath. These teachers dedicated their lives to the continuation and preservation of the lineage of Ashtanga yoga which had, in turn, given my life meaning. The spiritual learning that defined my life's purpose was rooted deeply within Ashtanga yoga as my teachers had taught me.

In Ashtanga Yoga there is no deity who will save you, but you can pray for one to clear the path ahead so you can walk with ease. For me, my teachers have been the instrument of divinity in the world. While the elephant god Ganesh never appeared to me, my teachers always did. Filled with gratitude for everything Guruji's presence had given me, my intention of traveling to Mysore this time was different. I was there to bring my teacher a present. The only gift fitting for a Guru that I could think of was gold.

The best and oldest jeweler in Mysore was called Bhima Brothers.

Located in the heart of Mysore city the store expanded to three full floors of intricate gold necklaces, bangles and rings. I took a rickshaw in to the beginning of Devarajurs Road, the main shopping street, and walked three blocks on the shady side of the street towards the jeweler's storefront. When I arrived the guard outside recognized me from previous visits, as did the owner, Mr. Bhima himself. He offered me chai and had one of his employees seat me in the air-conditioned showroom. When I explained that I was looking for a present for my teacher Mr. Bhima suggested a gold chain. This seemed appropriate as, of the many times that I had practiced with Guruji, he would often wear gold. After browsing through what felt like hundreds of chains I settled on one.

As I descended down the steps to hail a rickshaw and return to Gokulam I felt like I was carrying my heart in a tiny package. Later that afternoon I arrived at the gates of the New Shala with a navy blue velvet jewelry box in hand, hiding a shiny new gold link chain imbued with every ember of my heart. I stood at the footsteps of the stairs hesitant, not wanting to walk in. I waited, I fretted, I hemmed and hawed. Then with attentive, calm, openhearted awareness I walked up the stairs. Each clink of the rising elevation echoed in my joints. I felt each muscle, tissue, and organ; I felt my emotions rise and fall, bounce and crack. The varnished wooden doors that had so often served as a background for Guruji's body, face and presence were empty. The guards who recognized me smiled and waved, saying "Hello madam". I returned their greeting in silence.

In the marble lobby I peered again into the practice space, seeing extra-large photos of Krishnamacharya, Guruji and other important images. The colorful rugs smoked with the vibration of hundreds of yoga practitioners daily work. The fumes were still fresh in the empty air. My bare feet stepped into the practice space I knew so well.

A thinner, older-looking man stood before me wrapped in woolen hats, sweaters and scarves. "Guruji" I said and smiled. Looking my direction, he replied, "Mmmm, yes, you come." I walked into the office to find him moving towards his desk. I handed him the little navy blue box that held my heart in it. Known for tossing presents aside, he opened it immediately, which surprised me. I was excited and nervous, hopeful that he would appreciate the thought, even though it could not compare with other, more opulent gifts he had received from students. He tore open the wrapping and unpacked the box which revealed a sparking glimmer of gold in the afternoon light. Holding it up and keeping the chain steady in his gaze he looked at me and smiled. I hoped that his smile contained the recognition of my gratitude, love and devotion for him.

We spoke briefly about his health, which was not good, and his planned trips to Florida. A very dedicated student had built Guruji a yoga shala in Islamorada to honor his life's work. There was a visit to the Florida Keys scheduled where he intended to bless and initiate a new yoga shala. I was humbled and excited to think that I might see my teacher in Florida and share his presence with so many students who perhaps could not make the journey to India. The joy that had been his hallmark trait was only more present. The light in his eyes had not diminished one bit, though his age had made his body frail. On my knees I touched his now smaller, woolen-socked feet, saying "Thank you, Guruji" one last time. I rose to receive a hug, no kiss anymore (infection spreads easily through the lips), a pat on the back and a final "Mmm, good. Oh, thank you very much."

I walked out to share a casual conversation with Sharath about the Old Shala, the New Shala, the hundreds of students in Mysore, the growing number of students at my center in Miami, his new baby, my marriage to Tim and my first trip to Mysore. With tears I could no longer avoid, I wandered outside, down the streets of Gokulam that had been the stage for some of my life's deepest lessons. I climbed the steady incline to the end of the road with reflective eyes set on the path ahead.

I thought of the many lessons of yoga, remembering how every hard and challenging yoga posture offers spiritual peace in a demanding moment and how every moment creates new openings into spiritual truths. I was reminded that in order to be truly beautiful we sometimes have to see just how ugly we've been along the way.

After many years of practice, just as Guruji told me, a true and lasting peace settled deep within. Yoga had helped me fall deeper into a complete "yes" to the sacredness of life that exists all around. I never dreamed I would be married, a vegetarian or an early riser. Yet there I was, back in India with all of these things and happy. Through the muddy waters of my own vanity the seeds of an eternally graceful lotus flower were planted.

* * *

I traveled back to Mysore in January 2009 for five weeks of practice. I felt that I needed the time to be a student again and rekindle a spark of inspiration. I wished for a moment when I would experience the light of my teacher's presence again. In the yoga tradition there is a notion called Darshan, which means the sharing of the light. Sitting in Guruji's presence had been about sharing the inner spiritual light of yoga. It is the spiritual light that removes the darkness of illusion so the eternal truth within is revealed. The Ashtanga Yoga method says that when this light has traveled along the inner body and reached the center of the head, the crown chakra, known as Sahasrara, is awakened. This lotus flower of a thousand petals is the insignia of final liberation and its iconography is contained with the opening mantra chanted at the beginning of every Ashtanga Yoga class.

When I arrived in Mysore again I could feel a shift as though the light had changed or was fading. Guruji was not in his office any longer, nor was he sitting in his chair in the yoga room. He was, instead, mostly confined to his bedroom and rarely visited with anyone outside of his family circle. I accepted the lighter, younger energy and enjoyed the depth and power of the pure Ashtanga Yoga method while trying to remain non-attached to the past. Sharath was my yoga teacher during this trip and I enjoyed the connection that I felt with him.

Seeing Guruji's chair in the yoga shala empty most days I was reminded of the first days I spent practicing in the new shala on my second trip to India. When the space first opened Guruji. Sharath and Saraswati all sat on flimsy plastic chairs. During one of the first practices I looked up and saw Guruji sitting in this off-white piece of furniture that looked like it belonged to a cheap patio than a yoga master. I remember thinking the simple thought that he should have a nice chair, a throne really if that was possible. After practice that day I shared my thought with two friends, Eagle and Kishan, to see if they would help organize the project. That afternoon I asked Sharath if it would be ok for us to buy Guruji a chair and he said yes so the process began. We collected close to 20,000 rupees from the yoga students who were more than happy to donate for this cause. Within one week a wide wooden chair with carved arm-rests and a soft cushion was ready. Eagle and Kishan carried the chair into Conference on one Sunday in February 2003, just a little over a month after the New Shala opened. From now on his chair would be filled more with the energy of his presence than his physical form. As though accepting a place in the succession of teachers a statue of Patanjali sat behind Guruji's chair. On days that Guruji wasn't there Sharath never sat in his grandfather's place but moved his own humble office chair, slightly upgraded from plastic, to the front of the stage. Rather than a vacuum left unfilled this was more evident of the progression of yoga through a lineage of teachers into the present day.

On my last night in February one of my closest friends asked if we could go and see Guruji. Saraswati, his daughter, led us upstairs into Guruji's bedroom where he was resting. As soon as she explained that two yoga students were there to pay their respects he mustered all the force possible and brought himself to sit at the bedside. Dramatically paler, thinner and more frail than I ever thought possible my teacher sat shrouded in light. He recognized me as the "Miami" lady. We stayed only seconds. I touched his feet in honor of my Guru one last time. Saraswati guided us downstairs and I walked out of the shala.

The taxi ride into Bangalore airport and the two day journey back to Miami gave me time to contemplate the message that I wanted to share as I returned to teach workshops, retreats, and daily classes. I worked tirelessly. More than ever I believed that it was my dharma to inspire people to delve deep within themselves. I wanted to offer my life as service to tend the sacred fire of Ashtanga Yoga.

Then, on a Sunday in late May my teacher passed away. I almost lost the heart to practice that day but eventually managed to unroll my yoga mat and practice. Tim and I held a ceremony at Miami Life

Center the next day and traveled to India at the end of May to take part in the ceremony there. I found the ceremony incredibly moving. It commemorated the moment when Guruji reached Mahasamadhi, the deepest state of peace attainable after leaving the physical form. Hundreds of students gathered in Mysore to honor his life's work and his family organized a lunch with all of Guruji's favorite foods for everyone to partake in. I remember there were chapattis, dhal, rice, ghee and vegetable curries and while they all tasted wonderful, I could not really appreciate them without my teacher present. When we were done eating the servers each brought around a 5-rupee coin for each student—I admired the crescent and star on the front and rubbed my hands into the new nickel (I now carry the coin with me everywhere I go). After each student ate the blessed food we were allowed to enter, offer flowers and be a part of chanting ceremony that ended the days long puja to assure Guruji's safe passage in the afterlife according to traditional Brahmin guidelines.

We spent a week in India and then I sat on two airplanes to make the intercontinental travel that had become part of my daily routine. At London Heathrow I tried to distract myself with some mouth-watering pastries but it was no use. I couldn't help but feel that Guruji was the udder that guided the course of my life and without him I did not know where to turn. He believed in me more than I believed in myself and he ignited the sacred spiritual fire of yoga within my heart. He also introduced me to the notion of faith, which became a necessary component in my life. There is now a magical essence to the practice of yoga that has taken me through hidden doorways within my own body. An open mind, a courageous heart and a healed body have all been steps along the path of my own self-discovery. By using these three tools the movements of physical yoga have burned through negative behavioral patterns, released hidden pathways of energy and proven to illuminate the lives of everyone around me. Because of yoga, my life is forever in service to the lineage of Ashtanga Yoga.

I remember when I first stepped on a yoga mat, I had no understanding of the spiritual offerings it held. One thing that became evident through my first meeting with Guruji, a notion I have tried to clarify in this book, was that yoga isn't something to be measured by the attainment of postures, it is instead measured by devotion. Physical practice is never meant as ends in and of itself. To the contrary, the physical aspect is a tool that allows yoga practitioners to have an honest mirror of their inner world. Devotion is something we cultivate in the practice, for ourselves, our teacher and ultimately the Divine.

A student recently asked me what I thought the shelf life of a Mysore Style Ashtanga Yoga practitioner was. He was wondering if in my experience I saw that people were able to practice for a few months, a few years or even possibly a lifetime. While I have only been teaching for a little over ten years I have experienced and worked with a wide range of Ashtangis, from absolute beginner to lifelong practitioner. There is no absolute answer to this. Ideally yoga is a lifelong spiritual practice that helps students grow internally throughout their entire lifespan. It takes years before the deeper benefits of the practice really start to materialize. In the course of my teaching I've noticed that students who understand their yoga practice as a path to the realization of the divinity within have the faith, strength, peace and perseverance it takes to practice for their entire life. There is no end to the journey of yoga and in fact each practice offers yogis a new chance to realize even deeper levels of their inner self. Perhaps the greatest gift that yoga has to offer is the journey itself. After wandering into a yoga studio myself over a decade ago, my own life altering adventure began, taking me all over the world, from the heat and lush greens of Mysore, through the rich history of Europe, the grey skyscrapers of New York and countless other towns and cities. Ever since my first bend into downward dog, each passing day has widened my heart and filled me with such peace and joy. Yoga, in its purest form, has truly and utterly brightened the hours and seconds of my life. Through it, I have found my heart.

AFTERWORD

I returned to Mysore, India in February 2011 and January 2012 to practice at the K. Pattabhi Jois Ashtanga Yoga Institute with R. Sharath Jois. Much has changed and much has stayed the same. I intend to visit and continue my studies there as much as I can. On this recent visit I got to thinking about how, to a large degree, the heart of yoga is about non-attachment. For example, while I was blessed and lucky to experience the authenticity of Guruji's teaching at the Old Shala in Lakshmipuram I began to realize that I could not hold onto the experience. I had to let go, embrace the present and be eternally thankful for the time that I did have. A new era, a new energy and many new people were in Mysore to visit this now historic yoga city and I needed to open my heart to the teaching available in this new environment. This is how I try to live my life now—in the moment.

And so, for those readers with a desire to go to India or pursue any trip of personal spiritual study I encourage you to buy your airline ticket before you doubt yourself. Just jump, heart first, into the moment, into the light of spiritual fire. The rest will, honestly, work itself out.

Yoga is a personal practice that has the power to change your life, one practice, one posture, one breath at a time.

Be strong, be peaceful. Let yoga show you the way.

RECOMMENDED READING

Sri K. Pattabhi Jois,
Yoga Mala: The Original Teachings of Ashtanga Yoga.
(New York: North Point Press, 2010).

Edwin F. Bryant,
The Yoga Sutras of Patanjali.
(New York: North Point Press, 2009).

Guy Donahaye and Eddie Stern,
Guruji: A Portrait of Sri K. Pattabhi Jois Through the Eyes of His Students
(New York: North Point Press, 2010).

Suzuki Roshi,
Zen Mind, Beginner's Mind.
(Boston: Shambhala Publications, 2011).

Pema Chodron,
When Things Fall Apart: Heart Advice for Difficult Times.
(Boston: Shambhala Publications, 2002).

Jack Kornfield,
A Path with Heart: A Guide Through the Perils and Promises of Spiritual Life.
(New York: Bantam, 1993).

Brian L. Weiss, M.D.
Many Lives, Many Masters The True Story of a Prominent Psychiatrist, His Young Patient, and the Past-Life Therapy That Changed Both Their Lives.
(New York: Fireside, 1988).

Gabriel Cousens, M.D.
Conscious Eating.
(California: North Atlantic Press, 2000).

Robert Svoboda,
Prakriti: Your Ayurvedic Constitution.
(Wisconsin: Lotus Press, 1998).

Georg Feuerstein,
The Deeper Dimension of Yoga: Theory and Practice.
(Boston: Shambhala, 2003).

A. G. Mohan,
Krishnamacharya: His Life and Teachings.
(Boston: Shambhala, 2010).

Svatmarama,
The Hatha Yoga Pradiprika.
(New York: yogavidya,com 2002).

Candace B. Pert,
Molecules Of Emotion: The Science Behind Mind-Body Medicine.
(New York: Simon & Schuster, 1999).

Kendra Crossen Burroughs, Shri Purohit Swami and Andrew Harvey,
Bhagavad Gita: Annotated and Explained.
(Vermont: Skylight Paths, 2001).

Geometry, Measurement and Statistics 1
Implementation Guide

Written and developed by
Simon d'Angelo, Elizabeth Gibbs, Andrew Jeffrey,
Sue Lowndes and Dr Tony Wing

OXFORD

OXFORD
UNIVERSITY PRESS

Great Clarendon Street, Oxford, OX2 6DP, United Kingdom

Oxford University Press is a department of the University of Oxford. It furthers the University's objective of excellence in research, scholarship, and education by publishing worldwide. Oxford is a registered trade mark of Oxford University Press in the UK and in certain other countries.

First Edition published in 2014

ISBN 978-0-19-838943-9

10 9 8 7 6 5 4

Typeset by Tech-Set Ltd, Gateshead

Paper used in the production of this book is a natural, recyclable product made from wood grown in sustainable forests. The manufacturing process conforms to the environmental regulations of the country of origin.

Printed in China by Leo Paper Products Ltd

Acknowledgements
Written and developed by Simon d'Angelo, Elizabeth Gibbs, Andrew Jeffrey, Sue Lowndes and Dr Tony Wing

Cover photograph by Damian Richardson

Photographs by Damian Richardson, except: p.5, p.6, p.7: Chris King; p.15, p.24, p.42, p.68: Jonty Tacon; p.30: Suzy Prior

Technical artwork by Tech-Set Ltd, Gateshead

With special thanks to: Braunston Church of England Primary School, Northamptonshire; Francis Askew Primary School, Kingston-upon-Hull; Georgian Gardens Primary School, Rustington; Mill Lane Community Primary School, Oxfordshire; New End Primary School, Camden; Peacehaven Infant School, Brighton; Telscombe Cliffs Community Primary School, Peacehaven; Sonning Common Primary School, Banbury; St Bartholomew's Church of England Primary School, Brighton; St Michaels Church of England Primary School, Oxford; Tetsworth Primary School, Oxfordshire; Wheatley Church of England Primary School, Oxfordshire; Yewtree Primary School, Hertfordshire

The authors and publisher would like to thank all schools and individuals who have helped to trial and review Numicon resources.

www.oxfordprimary.co.uk/numicon

About Numicon

Numicon is a distinctive multi-sensory approach to children's mathematical learning that emphasizes three key aspects of doing mathematics: communicating mathematically, exploring relationships, and generalizing.

Numicon was founded in the daily experience of intelligent children having real difficulty with maths, the frequent underestimation of the complexity of the ideas that young children are asked to face when doing maths and recognition of the importance of maths to them and to society as a whole.

Numicon aims to facilitate children's understanding and enjoyment of maths by using structured imagery that plays to children's strong sense of pattern. This is done through research-based, multi-sensory teaching activities.

Numicon takes into account the complexity of abstract number ideas and seeks to foster the self-belief necessary to achieve in the face of challenge or difficulty.

Through the combination of communicating mathematically (being active, talking and illustrating), exploring relationships and generalizing, children are given the support to structure their experiences: a vital skill for both their mathematical and their overall development.

A multi-sensory approach, particularly one that makes use of structured imagery, provides learners with the opportunity to play to their strengths, thereby releasing their potential to enjoy, understand and achieve in maths. By watching and listening to what children do and say, this enjoyment in achievement is also shared by teachers and parents.

Numicon strives to support teachers' subject knowledge and pedagogy by providing teaching materials, Professional Development and on-going support that will help develop a better understanding of how to encourage all learners in the vital early stages of their own mathematical journey.

Contents

Welcome to Geometry, Measurement and Statistics 1

Before you start teaching, we recommend you take some time to familiarize yourself with the Numicon starter apparatus pack A, the teaching resources and the pupil materials, to help you and the children get the most out of using Numicon.

Use this Implementation Guide:

- to find out more about what Numicon is
- to find out how using Numicon might affect your teaching of geometry, measurement and statistics
- to learn about the key mathematical ideas children face in the Geometry and Measurement activity groups.

You will find more information, videos, ideas and free resources on the Numicon website: www.oxfordprimary.co.uk/numicon. Here you can sign up for our newsletter, which includes suggestions for topical mathematics and updates on Numicon.

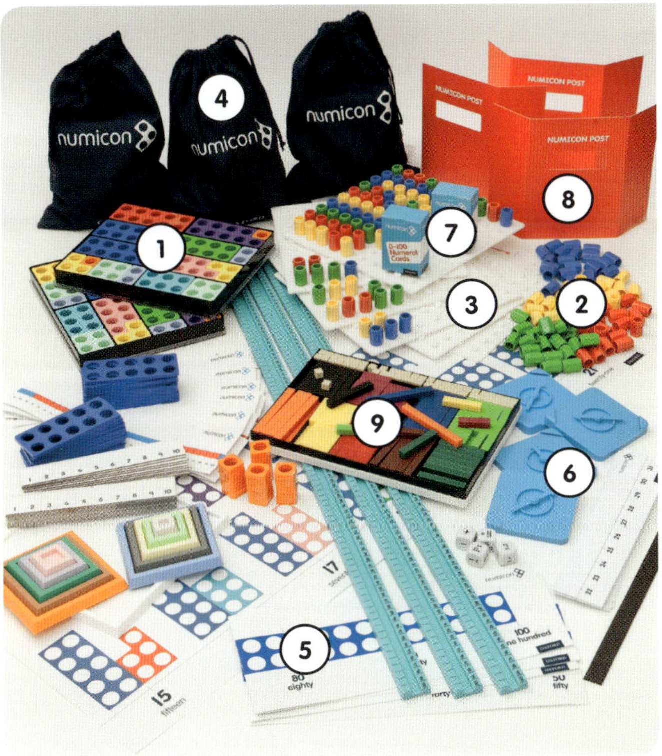

What's in the Numicon starter apparatus pack A?

The following list of apparatus supports the teaching of Geometry, Measurement and Statistics 1. These resources should be used in conjunction with the focus and independent activities described in the activity groups.

Apparatus pack contents

- Numicon Shapes – box of 80 (× 2)
- Numicon Coloured Pegs – bag of 80 (× 2)
- Numicon Baseboard (× 6)
- Numicon Feely Bag (× 3)
- Numicon 10s Number Line (× 3)
- Numicon Spinner (× 4)
- Numicon 0–100 Numeral Cards (× 2)
- Numicon Post Box – set of 3
- Number rods – large set
- Numicon 1–100 cm Number Rod Track (× 3)
- Numicon 0–100 cm Number Line – set of 3 (× 2)
- Extra Numicon 10-Shapes – bag of 10 (× 2)
- Extra Numicon 1-Shapes – bag of 20

The following apparatus is not specifically listed for use in Geometry, Measurement and Statistics 1 activities, but should be used freely and as needed to support and extend children's work.

- Numicon Display Number Line
- Numicon 0–31 Number Line – set of 3 (× 2)
- Numicon Number Rod 1–10 and 20 Trays
- Numicon Dice – set of 4
- Numicon 1–100 Card Number Track (× 2)
- Magnetic strip

Numicon Shapes 1

These offer a tactile and visual illustration of number ideas, and are used to support work on transformations and money in Geometry, Measurement and Statistics 1.

Numicon Coloured Pegs 2

These red, blue, yellow and green Pegs are useful for making patterns and arrangements and work on position and movement on a Baseboard.

Numicon Baseboard 3

The square Baseboard has 100 raised studs to hold Numicon Shapes and Pegs. It is used in many activities, providing a defined 'field of action' for reflection, rotation, position and movement and money work.

Numicon Feely Bag 4

By feeling for geometrical shapes in the Feely Bag, children visualize their parts and properties, helping them to develop their own mental and tactile imagery of 2D and 3D shapes.

Numicon 10s Number Line 5

This number line shows Numicon 10-Shapes laid horizontally end to end and marked with multiples of 10 from 0 to 100. It helps children to develop a 'feel' for the cardinal value of numbers to 100 and connect this to place value.

Numicon Spinner 6

Different overlays (provided as photocopy masters) can be placed on the Numicon Spinner to generate a variety of numbers, coin values, shapes and movement instructions.

Numicon 0–100 Numeral Cards 7

The pack of 0–100 Numeral Cards may be used in activities to generate numbers for children to work with. It is also used in some whole-class and independent practice activities.

Numicon Post Box 8

A card 'post box' through which Numicon Shapes, geometrical shapes and cards showing measurements (for example) can be posted.

Number rods 9

A set of ten coloured rods, 1 cm square in cross section. The shortest is 1 cm in length, the longest 10 cm. These offer another structured illustration for number. Being centimetre-scaled, they can also be placed along the Numicon 0–100 cm Number Line, and are used later in Geometry, Measurement and Statistics 2 to introduce centimetres as a unit of length.

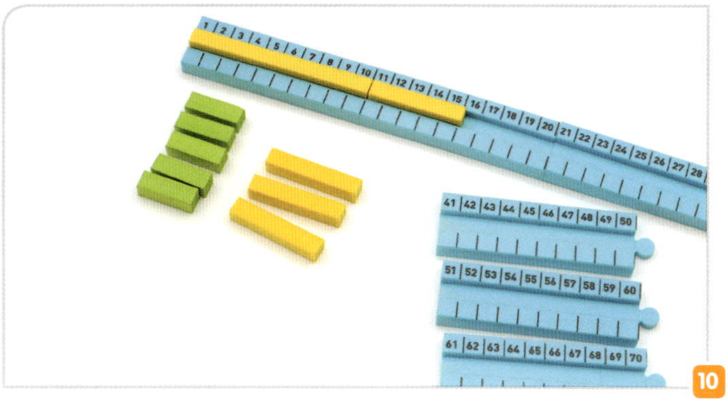
10

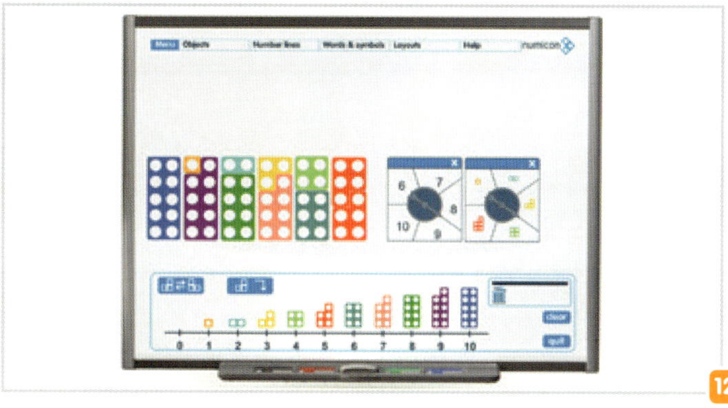
12

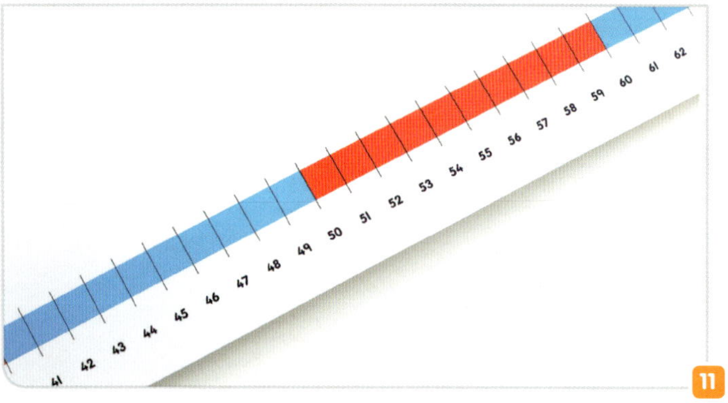
11

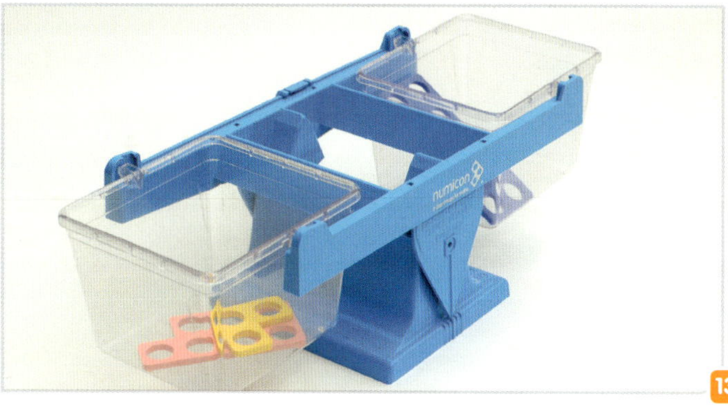
13

Numicon 1–100 cm Number Rod Track 10

The 1–100 cm Number Rod Track supports children's use of number rods and measurement work. The decade sections click together into a metre-long track and can also be separated into sections to form an array.

Numicon 0–100 cm Number Line 11

The points on this number line are 1 cm apart and are labelled from 0 to 100. The number line is divided into decade sections, distinguished alternately in red and blue. It can also be used with number rods, as an alternative to the 1–100 cm Number Rod Track.

Numicon Display Number Line

The Numicon Display Number Line provides a visual reference for children, connecting Numicon Shapes, numerals and number words with the number line.

Numicon 0–31 Number Line

This number line shows the numerals 0–31, spaced so that children can place a counter on each numeral in independent counting activities. It can be used to support children's number work in any context, as needed.

Numicon Number Rod Trays 1–10 and 20

This set comprises a Number Rod Tray for each number up to 10, plus one for 20. They can be used for exploring and building patterns.

Numicon Dice

A set of four 22 mm dice, featuring Numicon Shape patterns alongside the numerals: two 0–5 Dice, one 5–10 Dice and one +/– Dice. They can be used to generate numbers, calculations and instructions.

Numicon 1–100 Card Number Track

This number track is divided into ten strips, numbered 1–10, 11–20, 21–30, and so on. The sections can be arranged end to end horizontally or as an array similar to a 100 square. It can be used to support number work in any context.

Magnetic strip

This self-adhesive magnetic strip can be cut into pieces and stuck onto Numicon Shapes or number rods so that they can be used on a magnetic whiteboard.

Available separately

Numicon Software for the Interactive Whiteboard 12

This rich interactive tool is designed for use with the whole class to introduce key mathematical ideas. It includes: number lines featuring the Numicon Shapes, the Numicon Pan Balance, shapes, coins, Numicon Spinners and much more.

Numicon Pan Balance 13

Using Numicon Shapes, number rods or other objects in this adjustable Pan Balance enables children to see equivalent combinations. Children can easily see what is in the transparent pans, making the Pan Balance especially useful for comparing quantities as part of measurement work. It can also be used, in the same way as any bucket balance, to explore the concepts of 'heavier' and 'lighter' in Geometry, Measurement and Statistics 1.

Individual sets of Numicon Shapes 1–10

In Geometry, Measurement and Statistics 1 children can use these to help them in handling numbers as part of measurement work, and they are especially useful for introducing coins, helping children to link each coin with its value in pounds or pence.

Other equipment recommended for the teaching of geometry and measurement

The activities in Geometry, Measurement and Statistics 1 also make use of other resources which are typically found in classrooms and widely available from suppliers. Resources which are particularly useful for geometry and measurement activities are described in more detail here. Other, more generally useful items, such as sorting equipment, interlocking cubes, string, squared paper and so on, are highlighted in the '**Have ready**' sections of the focus and practice activities.

Pattern blocks 14

Pattern blocks are a size-matched set of shapes which children can use flexibly to explore and understand the parts and properties of 2D shapes. They can be used to make pictures and patterns during play, as well as to investigate, for example, how shapes can be combined to build other shapes or tilings, or to make repeating or symmetrical patterns.

Photocopy masters 19–24 provide cut-out pattern blocks based on a side length of 2·5 cm.

Geo strips and connectors 15

By connecting geo strips – flexible, punched strips of various lengths – children can make, alter and remake shapes for themselves, helping them to link the physical, variable properties of their models to concepts of space, line, angle and shape.

Photocopy masters 10 and 11 provide a cut-out template for making geo strips, which can be laminated for durability and used with paper fasteners.

Geoboards and elastic bands 16

Stretching an elastic band around the pegs on a geoboard is a quick and simple way for children to make and alter shapes, allowing them to explore a variety of geometric concepts, including angles, symmetry, area and perimeter, transformations, and coordinates, among others. Children's ideas and results can also be recorded onto matching 'dot' paper, making the geoboard a very useful investigative tool.

A number of types of geoboard are available, the most common of which has a square grid of pegs. Others are available in an 'isometric' arrangement which can be used to illustrate equilateral triangles and a wide variety of 3D shapes in particular. Note that isometric 'dot' paper can be used for recording in this instance.

Geometric shapes 17

A variety of images and examples of geometric shapes should be available for children to look at, handle and talk about during their play and work. Both flat, 2D shapes – including squares, oblongs, triangles and circles – and solid, 3D shapes – including cubes, cuboids, pyramids, prisms, cylinders, spheres and cones – should be presented in a variety of sizes, forms and contexts. You can also provide images and examples in context, to encourage children to notice the shapes they come across in everyday objects.

Programmable robots

A number of different programmable floor robots for classroom use are available. These require the user to enter a series of instructions, typically for turns and straight-line movements, which they follow to complete a journey around the floor. They represent a practical and appealing context for demonstrating, thinking about and experimenting with position, direction and movement, angles and turns, and measurement, among other topics, as well as for problem solving and logical thinking more generally. They are also a means of encouraging children to begin making links between mathematics and ICT, and of approaching the idea of programming. Opportunities for their use are highlighted in the focus and practice activities.

Clocks

Clocks, clock faces and clock images are used to help children learn about time measurement and telling the time. In Geometry, Measurement and Statistics 1 children begin with clock faces with a moveable hour hand, illustrating the 12-hour cycle of 'o'clock' times. They later move on to showing these times on clock faces with both hands, and using the position of the minute hand on the dial to illustrate times 'half past' the hour. Geared clocks (or clock faces with geared hands) are needed to show the linked movement of the hour and minute hands.

Photocopy masters of clock faces are provided on pages 2 and 5 of the *Geometry, Measurement and Statistics 1 Teaching Resource Handbook*, for children to use as needed to illustrate and record their learning.

In addition, pictures and examples of a variety of different types and designs of clocks and watches are helpful in encouraging children to consider similarities and differences, and ultimately to generalize their skills in telling time. They are likely to be familiar with digital clocks from the time displays on many electronic devices and appliances, and where appropriate can begin to make links with the 12-hour cycle illustrated by the clock face. The digital 12-hour clock and simple Roman numerals are introduced in Geometry, Measurement and Statistics 3, and the digital 24-hour clock in Geometry, Measurement and Statistics 4.

Items and materials for measuring; measuring instruments

In Geometry, Measurement and Statistics 1, children choose and use their own units to explore length, heaviness and capacity; they might measure a distance in steps, for example, or a capacity in scoops.

For learning about mass/weight, real-life objects for weighing are needed, including some which challenge the idea that 'larger is heavier', for example a large box of popcorn (large but light) or a paperweight (small but heavy). Children use balance scales to begin comparing masses more precisely, then move on to using standard units of mass in Geometry, Measurement and Statistics 2. It is useful to provide a variety of examples and images of balance scales, if possible, to help broaden children's experience.

The activities exploring capacity make use of water, and children will therefore need access to a suitable space in which to work with water and a water supply, along with other water-handling equipment, as appropriate – for example buckets, water trays, funnels and protective clothing. Alternatively, dry materials which pour, such as sand or rice, could be used. A large variety of containers – jugs, bottles, pots, cups, scoops, bowls, beakers, and so on, in a wide range of sizes and shapes – is also needed.

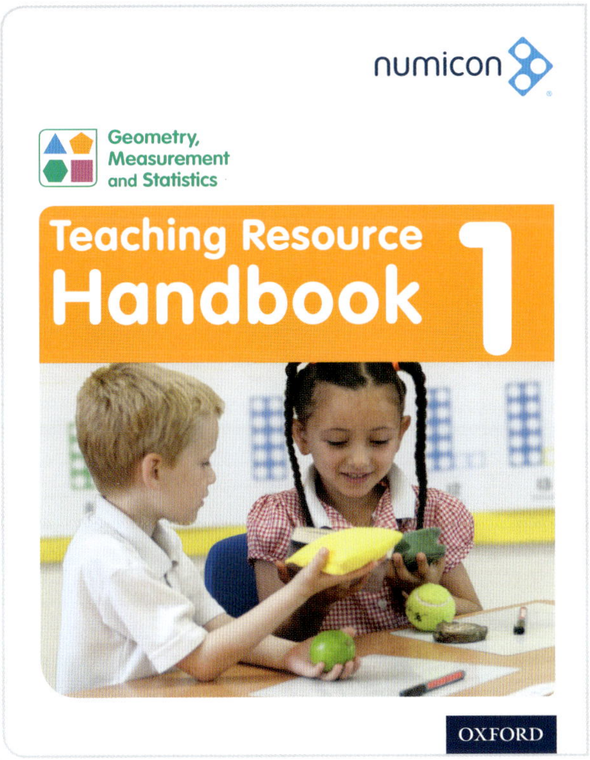

18

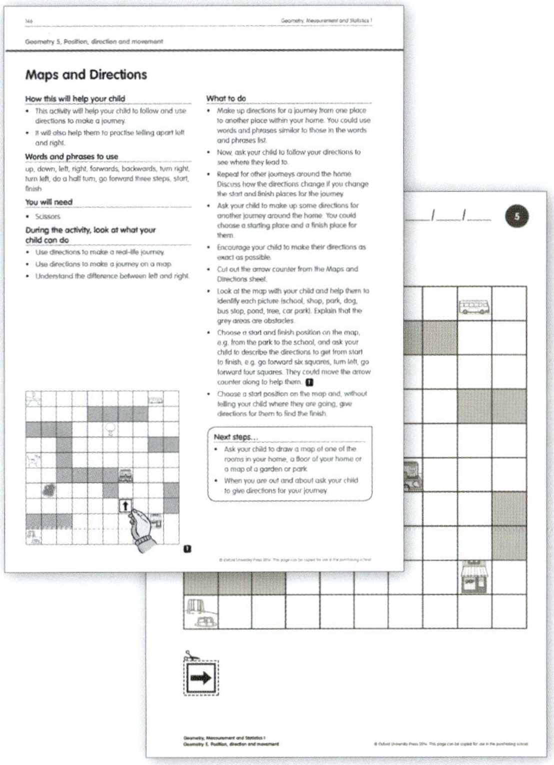

19

What's in the Numicon teaching resources?

Geometry, Measurement and Statistics 1 Teaching Resource Handbook 18

This contains 11 activity groups clearly set out and supported by illustrations. Each activity group begins with the educational context, learning opportunities, assessment opportunities and important mathematical vocabulary. To support teachers' assessing of children, there are notes on what to 'look and listen' for as children work on the activities, as well as suggestions for whole-class and independent practice. Photocopy masters supporting the 11 activity groups are included at the back of the Teaching Resource Handbook.

Support for planning and assessment is included in the front of the handbook. There, you will find:

- information on how to use the Numicon teaching materials and the physical resources
- long- and medium-term planning charts that show the recommended progression through the activity groups
- an overview of the activity groups.

Geometry, Measurement and Statistics 1 Explore More Copymasters (provided in the Teaching Resource Handbook) 19

The Explore More Copymasters offer children the chance to practise and discuss mathematics at home with a parent or carer. An activity has been included for each activity group so that children have ongoing opportunities to practise their mathematics learning outside of the classroom.

Each activity is supported by information for the parent or carer on the mathematics that has been learned in class beforehand, and the learning point of the activity itself. Guidance on how to complete the activity is included, as well as a suggestion for how to make the activity more challenging or how to further develop the activity in a real-life situation.

The Explore More Copymasters can be given to an adult or child as a photocopied resource.

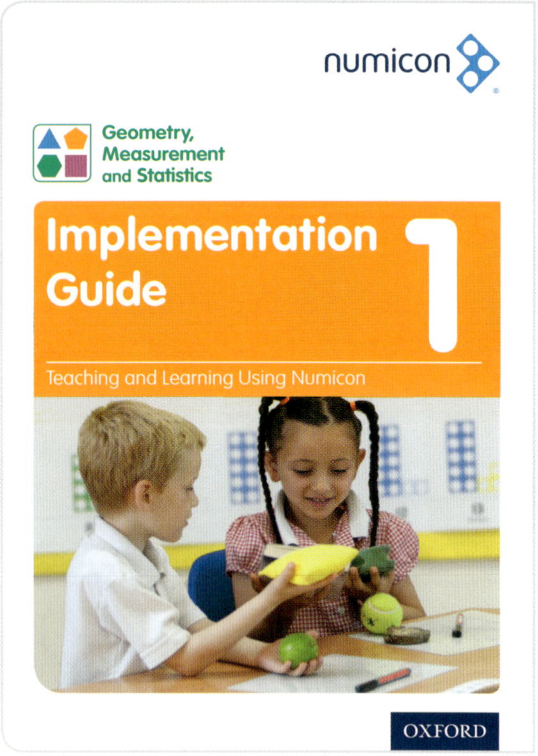

20

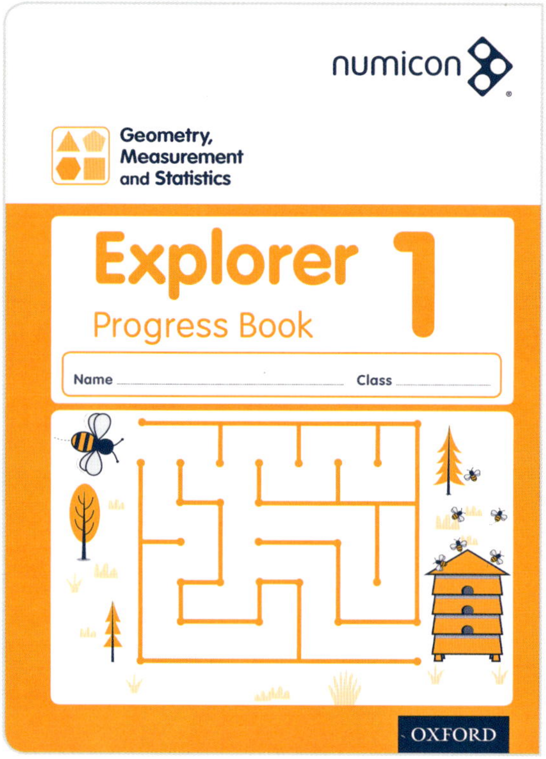

21

Geometry, Measurement and Statistics 1 Implementation Guide 20

This introduces what Numicon is and how Numicon helps children meet the demands of learning mathematics. It also includes some practical advice about what to do when preparing to teach with Numicon and answers some key questions about how to use Numicon in practice. The sections on 'Key mathematical ideas' provide useful explanations of the important concepts children will meet in 11 activity groups of the Teaching Resource Handbook and how these ideas develop when teaching with Numicon.

The different sections of the Implementation Guide can be accessed as and when necessary to help you with your teaching.

Geometry, Measurement and Statistics 1 Explorer Progress Book 21

The Explorer Progress Book offers children the chance to try out the mathematics they have been learning in each activity group. In children's responses, teachers will be able to assess what progress individual children are making with the central ideas involved in every activity group. It should be stressed that the challenges in the Explorer Progress Book are not tests. There are no 'pass/fail' criteria; the challenges are simply designed to reveal how well children can use the mathematics they have been learning in a new situation.

Being able to use mathematics in an unfamiliar situation is a significant indicator of children's understanding. Many of the tasks set mathematics in a new or different context and, where possible, the challenges are set in an 'open' way, inviting children to show how they can reason with the ideas involved, rather than testing they have learned a routine solution to routine tasks.

As with children's classroom activity work, a range of apparatus should be freely available to children as they reason with the ideas in their Explorer Progress Book.

In addition, there is also scope for self-assessment. This can be used flexibly throughout a term, or to summarize learning at the end of a block of work.

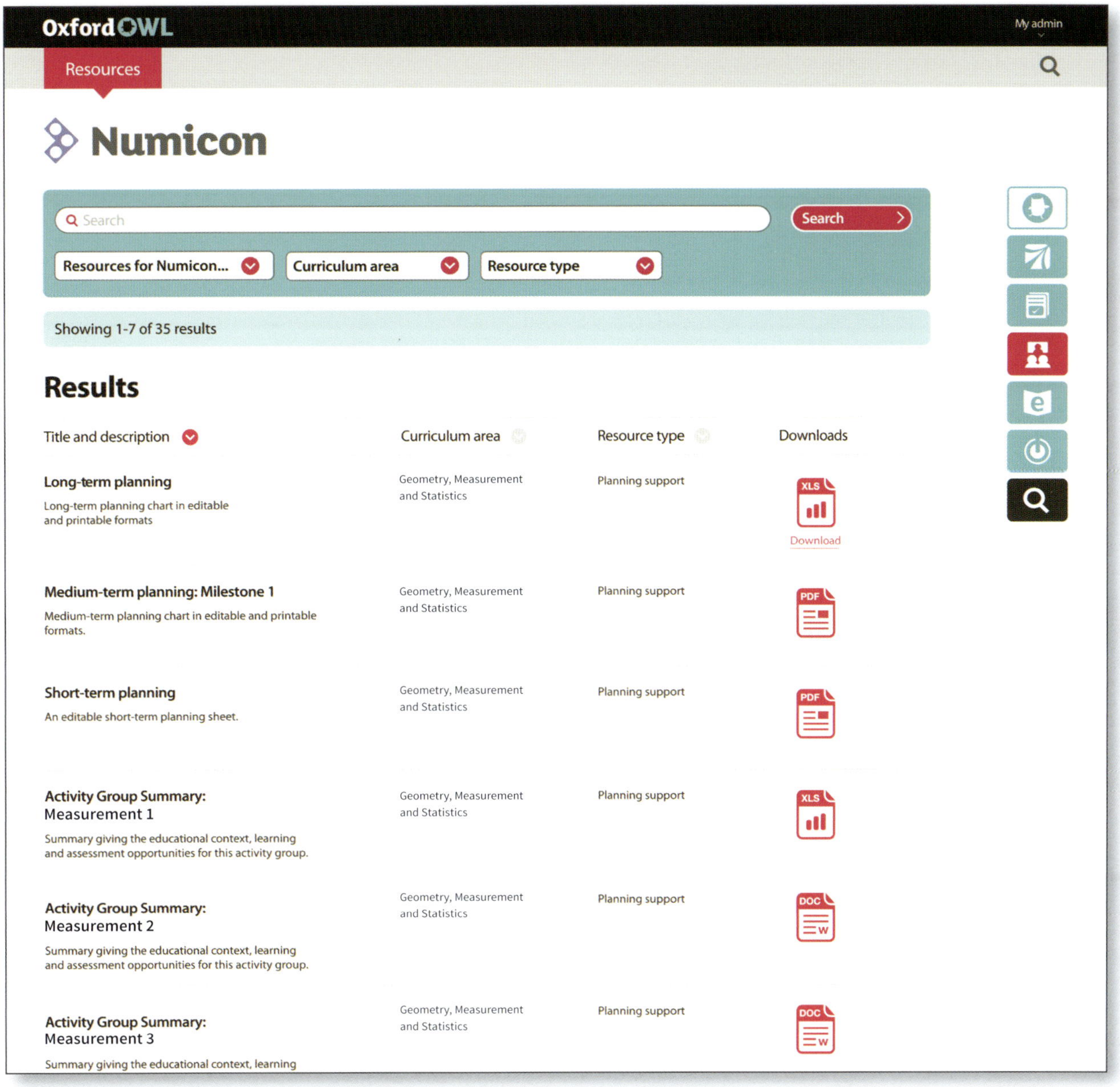

Numicon Planning and Assessment Support

The Numicon Planning and Assessment Support is designed to be used flexibly within schools' own planning formats. Within the support you will find short videos introducing Geometry, Measurement and Statistics 1 and offering advice that will help you get started with teaching with Numicon.

There is also an editable summary of each activity group, including the title and number of the group, the educational context, learning opportunities, assessment opportunities and the mathematical words and terms to be used with children as they work on the activities. There are suggestions for how to use these activity group summaries in your planning, as well as editable short-, medium- and long-term planning frames.

Assessment grids that support monitoring of children's work on the Explorer Progress Book and editable versions of the milestones for assessing children's progress are also available.

Charts that map Numicon to the English, Welsh, Scottish and Northern Irish curricula have been included in these resources, as have charts showing the progression of the Numicon teaching programme across Number, Pattern and Calculating and Geometry, Measurement and Statistics.

What is Numicon?

In order to illustrate how using Numicon in your teaching can help children learn mathematics, this section looks at:

- what Numicon is
- what doing mathematics demands of children
- how using Numicon helps children meet these unique demands.

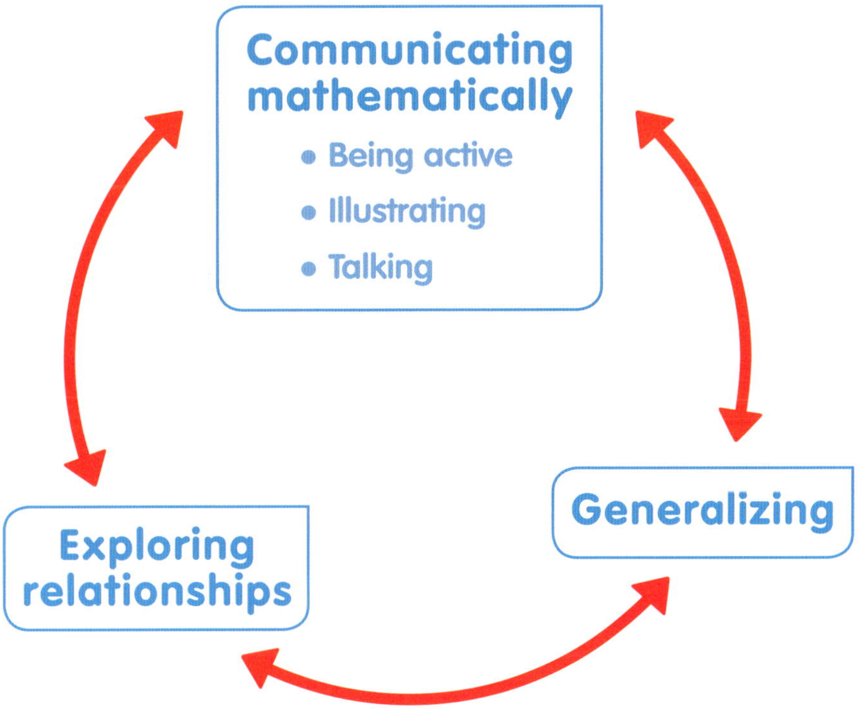

What is Numicon?

Numicon is a distinctive approach to children's mathematical learning that emphasizes three key aspects of doing mathematics: communicating mathematically, exploring relationships, and generalizing.

Communicating mathematically

Doing mathematics involves communicating and thinking mathematically – and these are two sides of the same coin. We think in the same ways that we communicate, and communicate in the same ways that we think. As children learn to communicate mathematically, they learn to think mathematically. This involves them in the following:

Being active: Teaching and learning with Numicon requires children to be active. This does not only mean being physically active (e.g. fitting physical objects together, finding a number on a number line, drawing a shape), but is a requirement reflecting the understanding that mathematics itself is activity: mathematics is something children are learning to *do*.

What this means in practice is that it is always the children themselves who are to do the mathematics. Telling children (or showing, or explaining) 'what to do' can encourage children to be passive. Numicon asks that the children do the mathematics, that is, both the activity and the thinking. In other words, children actively learn to do mathematics for themselves.

Illustrating: Doing mathematics, that is, thinking and communicating mathematically, necessarily involves illustrating, because mathematics is about studying relationships between objects, actions and measures, and it is impossible to explore such relationships without some kind of spatial imagery being involved. Even when thinking about just two numbers, one of them 'comes after' the other one on a number line or is said to be 'bigger' or 'higher'; these relations all involve spatial imagery.

Numicon explicitly involves illustrating in every activity. This is how relationships in a wide variety of contexts are both explored and communicated.

Talking: Since doing mathematics involves communicating mathematically (both with others and with ourselves), doing mathematics also involves talking. Talking is an essential aspect of all Numicon activity.

Throughout Numicon, talking means dialogue in which points of view are exchanged between teachers and children, and between children and children. All partners in dialogue will be actively involved, not just passively hearing, or waiting to speak. Such exchanges encourage reflective thinking as children learn to discuss different points of view, both with others and with themselves.

Exploring relationships (in a variety of contexts)

Doing mathematics involves **exploring relationships**, that is, the structure, in any situation in order to develop some kind of control in that area. Relationships can be between amounts, between positions, between shapes, between things that are varying, between things that are constant, or between combinations of all of these things. Fully understanding the relationships in a situation makes it predictable, thus making it possible to find out and/or manage what is needed. The mathematical reasoning children are asked to do is their expression of relationships they perceive.

Numicon ensures that children explore the relationships within a wide range of contexts so that they learn not only *how* to do mathematics, but *when* the mathematics they are learning is useful.

Generalizing

In doing mathematics, exploring relationships and looking for patterns in various situations lead to **generalizing**. It is generalizing that allows us to make whole ranges of new situations predictable.

Numbers are generalizations that we all use to make predictions when calculating. For example, the '6', '2' and '8' in the number sentence '6 + 2 = 8' are generalizations; 6 of anything and 2 of anything, will together always make 8 things, whatever they are.

'The angles of a triangle add up to 180°' is a generalization that is often used when doing geometry; 'the area of a circle is 'πr^2' is another that is used when measuring.

In each of these cases, noticing patterns in relationships allows us to generalize about an infinite number of other, similar situations.

It is because we make and use generalizations continually as we do mathematics that mathematical thinking and communicating will appear to have an abstract character for children if they are not involved in doing the generalizing for themselves.

Communicating mathematically, **exploring relationships** and **generalizing** all come together when *doing* mathematics.

What doing mathematics demands of children

In learning to do mathematics at the age they are asked to, children face a unique challenge in their school curriculum: thinking and communicating about abstract objects.

Pure numbers, such as 6 and 254, are abstract objects and in no other subject are children asked to work with and reason about such things so early. It is not surprising that children can hesitate, be puzzled, get stuck, or take time to work things out for themselves.

Most mathematicians will say that doing mathematics is about looking for patterns in situations. It is, but there is more to it than that. When you find a pattern, it means you have noticed something regular, something that always seems to be happening, and this means that any pattern you see is a generalization of yours. Mathematics deals almost entirely in generalizations.

Which is what numbers are: as generalizations, they are abstract objects. Very early on in mathematics, young children are asked to do things with lots of abstract objects, like those we call '3', and 'ten'. Not '3 pens', or 'ten sweets', or '3 friends'. Just '3', or, even more curiously, the two-digit '10' by itself. Notice how quickly children are asked to add and subtract these abstract objects to and from each other. There are high expectations of every child from the very beginning in mathematics.

The central problem: communicating with, and about, abstract objects

How is it possible to communicate about abstract objects? And, since thinking is communicating with ourselves, how is it possible to *think* about abstract objects?

Notice that 'abstract' does not mean 'imaginary'. We can easily picture imaginary things, such as unicorns and beings from outer space, but abstract things are different. Abstract things include qualities like 'truth', 'intelligence', 'common sense', as well as generalizations such as '6 of anything'. The problem is, as soon as you try to picture '6 of anything', you find you are imagining '6 of something'.

The answer, as Bruner observed, is that we think about abstract objects with symbols; in the case of numbers, we do it with numerals.

The important thing about symbols is that they do not attempt to show literally what is being talked about; they are simply arbitrary, conventional marks on a page (or spoken words). When what we are communicating about with these symbols is abstract, that absence of a picture is inevitable; how could we possibly picture something that is abstract?

It is easy to picture '3 pens' or 'ten friends', but what might the abstract '3' look like? Or, how about the curious two-digit '10'? Since numerals do not look like the abstract things they 'stand for', how are children to learn to interpret such arbitrary symbols in their thinking and communicating? Doing mathematics – thinking and communicating about abstract things with symbols – is certainly not easy for young children.

How does Numicon help?

Essentially, Numicon does two things. Firstly, Numicon acknowledges that in order to understand what numbers are, children have to generalize. Secondly, Numicon follows Bruner's advice in using children's actions and imagery to prepare for their use of mathematical symbols in their thinking and communicating. In practice, these two things are done at the same time.

In Bruner's terms, *enactive* and *iconic* representations (action and imagery) are used to inform children's interpretation of the *symbolic* representation (e.g. numerals) that is necessary for communicating their pattern spotting (generalizing). To aid children's necessary generalizing, strong focus is placed upon the use of structured materials.

Generalizing and reasoning – an early years example of teaching with Numicon

Initially, in common with most teaching, Numicon involves a wide variety of everyday objects (such as beads, cubes, pegs and counters, see Fig 1) in order to help children develop their counting, before then introducing the challenges of calculating.

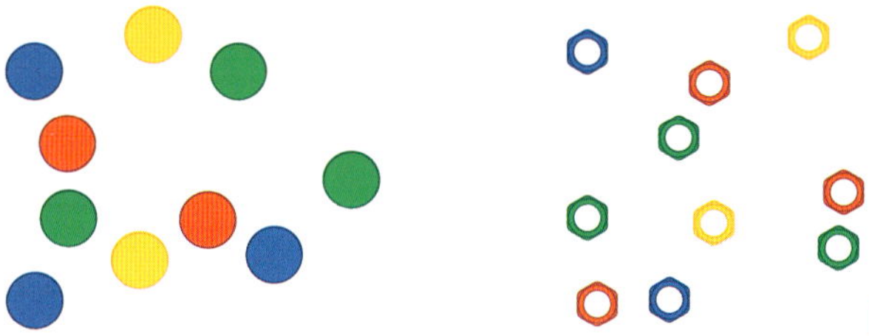

Fig 1

Importantly, Numicon also introduces sets of structured materials in which individual pieces have *regular* physical relationships with each other, for example, Numicon Shapes and number rods, see Fig 2. Children explore the physical relationships within these structured materials by, for example, ordering pieces, comparing them, combining them physically to make others.

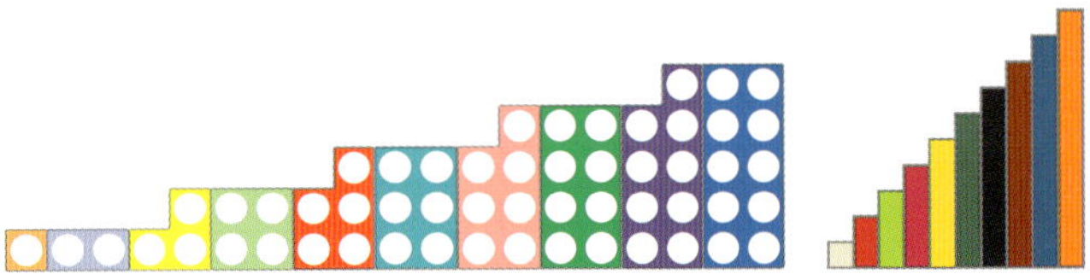

Fig 2

Thus, as children work with loose collections (beads, cubes) and with structured materials (Numicon Shapes and number rods), they are able to combine being active with physical objects and images as illustrations in their talking and thinking about numbers of things.

Numerals are introduced in association with loose collections of objects and with structured materials as children work; thus, symbolic representation appears alongside children's ongoing action and imagery with physical objects.

Number lines (e.g. Fig 3) are introduced to further illustrate the ordering that is evident within the structured materials, and to reinforce the associated ordering of numerals.

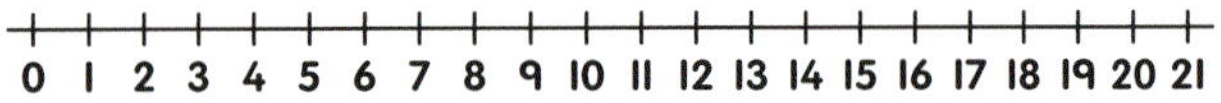

Fig 3

Importantly, loose collections of objects are arranged into the regular patterns of the Numicon Shapes; individual number rods are found to be equivalent in length to different multiples of the smallest 'unit' rod (e.g. Fig 4).

Fig 4

Through doing these activities, children learn that *any* collection of loose objects can be arranged into Numicon Shape patterns that can then be 'read'. Children learn to 'see' how many objects are in a collection without counting; numbers of things begin to 'take shape' visually, in organized ways.

It is now possible to prepare children for further generalizing about numbers through exploring relationships between numbers of things. Children's mathematical thinking and communicating continue to develop through their being active with the objects they are given, and in illustrating their talking about what they see and do.

Children generalize that any collection of loose objects can be arranged into Numicon Shape patterns. They also generalize that any number of 'unit' number rods may be exchanged for (will be 'as long as') one or more of the larger number rods. Thus *any* number of loose objects can be converted into (is equivalent to) one or more Numicon Shapes or number rods.

In realizing that any collection of loose objects can be arranged into Numicon Shape patterns, and that any number of unit

cubes is equivalent to one or more number rods, children become able to 'see the general' in any particular illustration; Numicon Shapes and number rods can be used to illustrate, in an organized way, any numbers of any kinds of things.

Numicon Shapes and number rods themselves may now be used to explore and to communicate about number relationships in general. They have become communication mediators in discussions about numbers and their relationships.

As a particular example, the Numicon Shape that has three holes fits together physically with the Shape that has five holes. The result 'forms the same shape as' (is equivalent to) the Shape that has eight holes, see Fig 5.

Similarly, the number rod worth three units, combined end-to-end with the rod worth five units, are together as long as the rod worth eight units, see Fig 6.

When laid end-to-end along a number line or number track, the '3 rod' and the '5 rod' together reach the position marked '8' on the line.

Fig 5

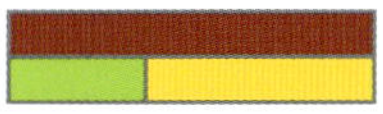

Fig 6

From these actions, and with these illustrations, children are able to generalize that: three *anythings* and five *anythings* together will *always* make eight things.

This generalization can be expressed using the numeric and verbal symbols: 3 and 5 together are equivalent to 8.

Later on, using further actions and further illustrations, children become able to interpret and use the further symbols '+' and '=' to express their generalization thus:

$$3 + 5 = 8$$

Importantly, at this stage children will have begun to use number words (one, two, three) as *nouns* instead of as adjectives (two sweets, three pencils) in their talking.

With their use of number words as nouns, numbers as *abstract objects* have now appeared in children's mathematical thinking and communicating, referred to with *symbols*.

Such generalizing and use of symbols can now be exploited further. If 'three of *anything*' and 'five of *anything*' together always make 'eight *things*', then:

3 tens + 5 tens = 8 tens
3 hundreds + 5 hundreds = 8 hundreds
3 millions + 5 millions = 8 millions

or

30 + 50 = 80
300 + 500 = 800
3,000,000 + 5,000,000 = 8,000,000

Such is the power of generalizations, and of the symbolic notation that children can by this stage use to think and communicate mathematically about them.

Progressing from such early beginnings

The foregoing example also illustrates how Numicon supports the teaching of children's subsequent mathematics.

In a wide variety of contexts, children are offered opportunities to be active and to illustrate their talking about any (and all) relationships they are exploring between both physical and abstract objects. They do this in order that they may generalize and, as a consequence, think and communicate about their generalizations with the conventional symbols of mathematics: in other words, that they may *do* mathematics.

Of course, there is much more beyond this first example. Children have many other relationships to explore, further generalizing to do, and thus many more conventional symbols to learn to interpret and use. However, wherever it is used, the approach is essentially the same. *Enactive* and *iconic* representation are used to inform children's interpretation of the *symbolic* representation that is necessary for thinking and communicating about their constantly developing pattern spotting (generalizing).

The going gets harder as children progress in their number work: place value, ratios, fractions, decimals and negative numbers will all challenge children's capacity to generalize onwards from these early beginnings. However, such advanced work is equally possible with the same approach of actions and illustrations building towards generalizing, and a consequent use of symbols to think and communicate about the generalized, abstract mathematical objects created. This is how the symbolism of mathematics becomes meaningful.

In their work on geometry, the generalizations that children reach in their mathematical thinking and communicating happen more gradually as they progress towards being able to reason about invented abstract objects such as 'any triangle' and (later) 'any polygon'.

It is impossible to draw the abstract object 'any triangle' in the same way that it is impossible to imagine 'six of anything'. As soon as you draw a triangle, however you have chosen to draw it, you have drawn a particular one; it does not matter whether you draw one that is right-angled, isosceles, equilateral, or scalene, what you have drawn is not a general triangle – it is a particular one, e.g. Fig 7.

Fig 7

However, as with generalizing about numbers, in doing geometry, much exploring of relationships with action and imagery (enactive and iconic representation) prepares children for reasoning meaningfully about 'any triangle' with symbolic representation (words and symbols).

In this example, as children physically construct and transform many varieties of triangles with dynamic materials, what they see before their eyes is how lengths of sides may vary endlessly as angles change, how angles may vary endlessly as lengths change and yet, despite all the variety they see, the shapes they are creating all turn out to be triangles.

Dynamic mental imagery deriving from these physical experiences then allows children to speak and to think of 'any triangle' as they imagine an infinitely flexible closed 2D shape with three straight sides.

By stressing the straightness of the sides, that there are always exactly three sides and that the sides fit together to 'close' the shapes they make, and by ignoring the constantly changing lengths of sides and sizes of angles, children become able to imagine 'any triangle' and to reason about it with words and symbols.

Then, having generalized to a stage when their mental imagery allows them to imagine and speak meaningfully about 'any triangle', children are in a position to further generalize that, for example, 'the angles of any triangle add up to 180°' through further action, imagery and reasoning with symbols.

In the same way that generalizing about numbers is approached, exploring relationships with action and imagery in geometry prepares children for reasoning meaningfully about abstract mathematical objects with symbols.

We reach all the generalizations of mathematics, and the symbols we use to express them, through being active and illustrating our talking about the relationships we are exploring.

Doing mathematics in the world – solving problems

Of course, *doing* mathematics in the everyday world is not simply about making generalizations and using symbols. Crucially, it also involves making *use* of generalizations to solve problems in particular situations.

For example, the generalization '4 x 25 = 100' allows us to predict that the perimeter of a square of side 25 cm will be 100 cm, that the area of a field measuring 4 m by 25 m will be 100 m^2, and that if you save £25 a week for four weeks you will have £100. It can also be very useful to help calculate that:

$$36 \times 25 = (9 \times 4) \times 25 = 9 \times (4 \times 25) = 900$$

Children need to be able to readily connect the generalizing that they do with mathematical symbols with everyday world situations in which those generalizations are useful.

In their more general problem solving, children learning, for example, *how* to divide one number by another, need to learn *when* that operation is useful.

The Numicon teaching materials organize activities into groups based around mathematical themes. For example, 'length' or 'rotation'.

The Numicon teaching materials organize activities into groups based around mathematical themes. For example, 'Length' or 'Position, direction and movement'.

In the activity group titled 'Comparing, ordering and measuring length' (Measurement 1), children start their exploration by talking about and comparing lengths in the context of a story. They begin measuring lengths by devising appropriate non-standard units to suit the context and available resources. They then move on to make use of this approach to solve problems involving different types of measurements of length, including width and distance.

In the activity group titled 'Position, direction and movement' (Geometry 5), the activities involve giving and following directions, helping children to expand and refine their knowledge and use of positional concepts and terms. They are given opportunities to experiment with size and direction of turn, and discover connections and equivalences, for example that a full turn is the same as two half turns. Later they move on to using board games, and begin to develop an understanding of position in relation to objects and shapes, and visual representations of these.

In these ways, children's mathematics is introduced, wherever possible, within contexts in which that mathematics is useful. Such contexts help children to 'see the point' of the mathematics they are learning, and prevent mathematics becoming a series of answers to problems they have never had.

Flexibility, fluency, and persistence

Being able to do mathematics effectively also includes being able to remember basic things such as those generalizations known as 'times tables' and number 'facts'. There are many practice activities built into the Numicon written materials that encourage children to develop a regular familiarity with basic facts.

Even more important to effective functioning is flexibility in mathematical thinking and communicating. Three kinds of flexibility are especially useful.

Through being active, children are able to 'invert' their actions; put more simply, this is about 'doing and undoing'. As children have found 'how many' objects there are in a collection by physically grouping them into tens (and hundreds), they are later readily able to 'partition' numbers ('undo' their groupings) when calculating with symbols.

As children can combine and separate Numicon Shapes and number rods physically ('do' and 'undo' their actions), they are able to connect adding and subtracting as inverse operations and to check a subtracting calculation by adding.

The introducing and encouraging of a variety of ways of calculating means that children are able to choose methods of calculating that suit the particular numbers involved, rather than adopting a standard method for any calculation. Who would want to subtract 1998 from 4673 using a column method, just because the numbers are big?

As Numicon approaches children's use of mathematical symbols with prior actions and imagery, if children become 'stuck' or hesitant while working with symbols, it is always possible for them to recall and return to the supporting activity and illustration from which their original generalizing arose. For example, if they are working on prime numbers, using symbols, they can immediately return to actively illustrating how factors 'go into' their various multiples physically with Numicon Shapes and with number rods. They can follow a similar pattern with any other kind of number relationship. This flexibility is one of movement backwards and forwards between Bruner's *enactive*, *iconic* and *symbolic* forms of representation in their thinking and communicating.

Finally, because Numicon continuously emphasizes communicating mathematically, it is possible to stress to children that all is not lost when they feel 'stuck'. The thing to do, always, when they 'don't know what to do' in a situation is to communicate.

Being active, illustrating and talking about the relationships we are exploring *is* doing mathematics. Persistence – an invaluable quality when doing mathematics – comes from continuing to communicate, with yourself and/or with others, whenever you cannot see where you are going.

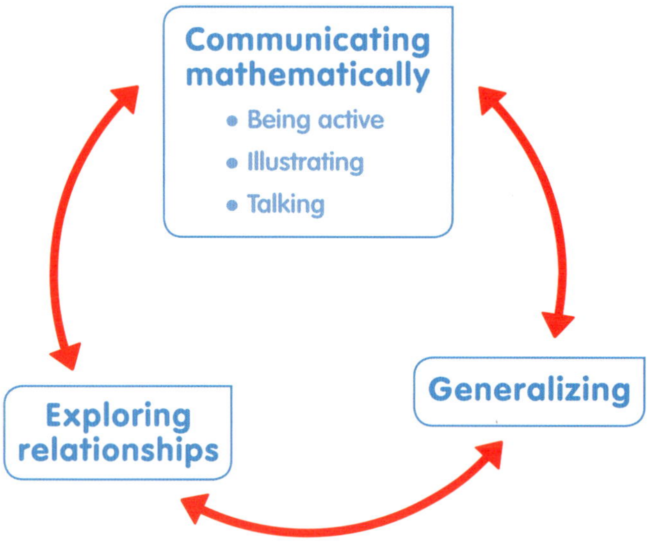

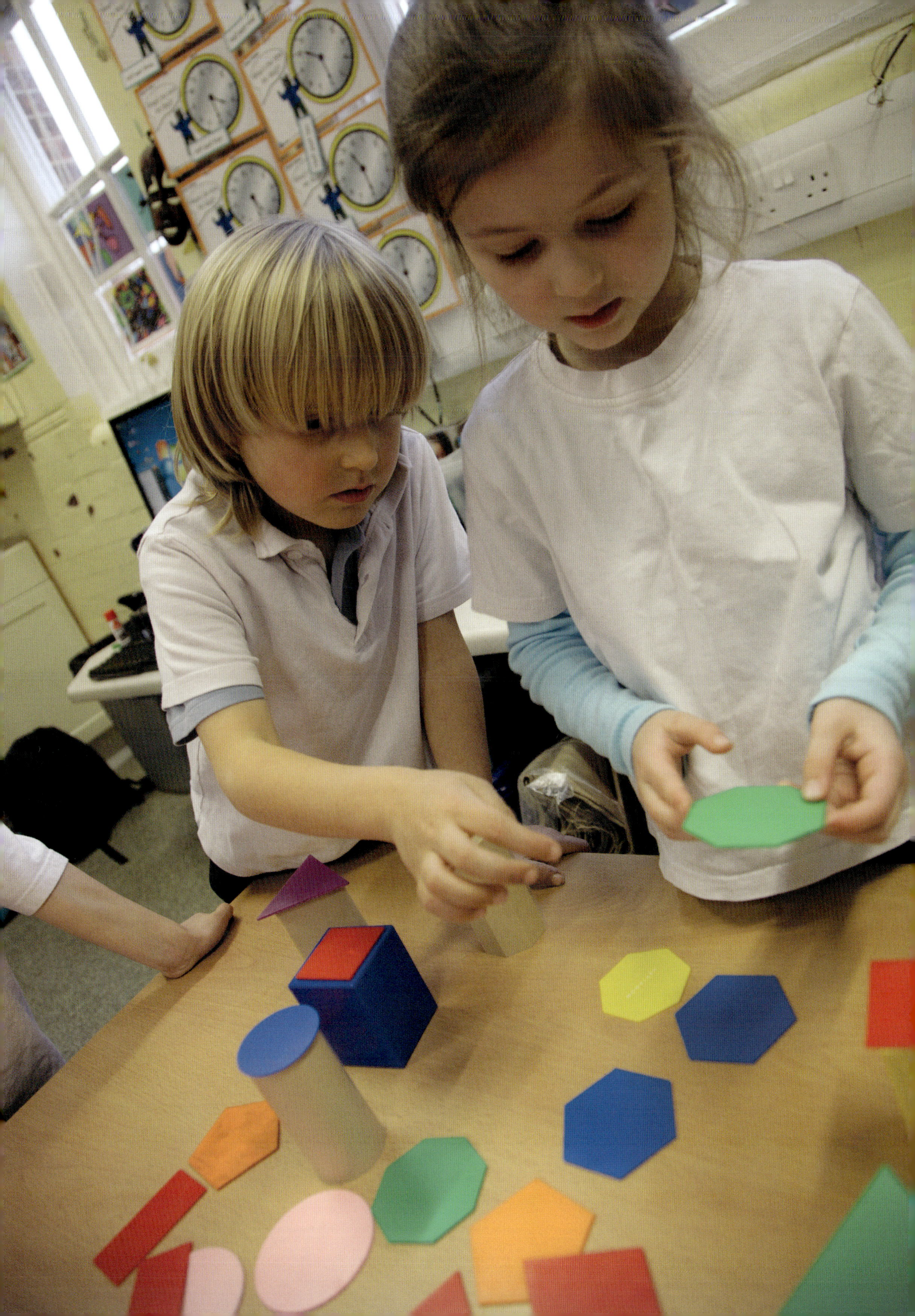

Preparing to teach with Numicon

This section is designed to support you with practical suggestions in response to questions about how to get started with Numicon in your daily mathematics teaching. It also contains useful suggestions on how to plan using the long- and medium-term planning charts as well as information on how to assess children's progress using the Numicon materials.

When getting started with Numicon, as well as reading this section, it can be helpful to refer to the suggested teaching progression in the programme of Numicon activities. This, along with the long- and medium- term planning charts, can be found in the *Geometry, Measurement and Statistics 1 Teaching Resource Handbook.*

How might using Numicon affect my mathematics teaching?

There will be a continual emphasis on communicating mathematically. Once involved in this communication process, children become active, in the sense that they become engaged in 'doing' mathematics for themselves. They begin to reflect on different points of view and to develop the imagery required to communicate mathematically, as well as the ability to illustrate their ideas.

For geometry and measurement, this imagery and illustration has a particularly active, practical foundation. Children develop and refine their thinking about shape, space and size through physical exploration – through making, comparing and manipulating objects. In their early work on measurement, for example, they might line up one object with another to show clearly which is 'longer', while in geometry they might learn to distinguish a rectangle from a parallelogram through handling and comparing examples, showing which have 'square' corners. In this sense, increasing dexterity and control of movement is another element of their developing skill in mathematical communication. As this communication becomes established as part of the culture of the classroom, children will increasingly join in conversations with you and their classmates. Mathematics lessons will develop into dialogue with ready use of imagery to illustrate ideas. A sense of shared endeavour will emerge as children solve problems through communication and persistence. So, when children feel 'stuck', they will know that the thing to do is to talk about it, to try to explain what the difficulty seems to be and to use illustrations and actions to express the problem. Careful questioning can encourage children to really think about 'difficulty' and to arrive at solutions gradually.

As the focus on mathematical communicating grows, you may become more aware of the words and terms you use in your teaching. It is important to use words and terms consistently. Try to encourage other adults in your class – and throughout the school – to use mathematical language consistently. Listen out for children using the same words and imagery to explain their ideas, though to start with they may use them only hesitantly.

In their work on geometry, for example, children begin to classify solid 3D shapes through reasoning about the parts and properties different examples have in common, making use of ideas and terms such as 'surface', 'corner' and 'edge'. They are encouraged to name these shapes for themselves, and to further refine the names as their reasoning develops. The terms 'cube', 'cylinder', and so on are then introduced in the context of giving instructions for making models, where use of agreed names for these generalized, abstract objects makes practical sense.

Similarly, in their work on measurement, children are first introduced to the use of a 'unit' of measurement in the context of length, and then begin to generalize this through their experiences in the areas of mass/weight and capacity. They are given the opportunity to further refine the concept through arriving at an understanding of the usefulness of an agreed, standard unit.

This increased focus on mathematical communicating will make it easier, through watching, questioning and listening to children as they work, to judge whether they are facing a suitable level of challenge. Activities are structured so

that at each stage children encounter a new 'problem' to solve – Numicon aims to encourage children to relish this, to persevere in working through any difficulty, to gain a sense of achievement when it is overcome, and to be excited about and ready to progress to the next challenge.

How can I encourage communicating?

Children respond to the examples around them. As such, the ways in which you communicate mathematically provide a model for children's communicating. Engaging in dialogue with children, actively listening to what they are saying and responding sensitively with thoughtful questions will encourage children to listen to one another and respect each other's ideas.

Make sure that appropriate resources for illustrating ideas in the area of study are freely accessible. For example, when studying length, interlocking cubes, lengths of string and straight edges (e.g. counting sticks, rulers) can be made available to children, or, for geometry, pattern blocks, geo strips, construction blocks, 2D and 3D shapes, interesting packaging and modelling dough.

Observe how children use these objects, listen to what they are saying, watch what they are doing and respond with questions and qualified praise when you notice active listening and thoughtful questioning. What children do and say will help you to understand what they are thinking.

The activities in Geometry, Measurement and Statistics 1 are designed to build on a foundation of understanding, skills and knowledge in the areas of number, pattern and calculating. Within the Numicon teaching programme, the 'Securing Foundations' section of *Number, Pattern and Calculating 1* provides this basis for mathematical development, and helps children make the transition from play-based activities to a daily mathematics lesson. It will also ensure children's familiarity with structured apparatus such as Numicon Shapes and number rods. Consistency in the use of resources and language across children's mathematics learning will, as already mentioned, help them to develop a solid framework within which to share and develop their ideas.

Providing a range of examples and contexts for children's work will also encourage them to develop and refine the imagery they use to 'do' mathematics. Opportunities are highlighted throughout the activities; for example, real-life paths, pavements and walls might be used to illustrate the idea of tiling (tessellation), while wallpaper, wrapping paper and fabric can be used to encourage children to appreciate different aspects of shape, repetition and pattern. Both images and actual objects might be used.

Finally, the ways in which children are grouped or paired for working together has an impact on their communicating, so this needs careful consideration.

Using daily routines to encourage communicating

A 'morning maths meeting', perhaps 15 minutes long, has proven to be very successful in encouraging children's mathematical communicating.

These meetings are oral and practical and include a small selection of key routines in which children practise rapid recall and gain fluency with the ideas and facts that are the basis or focus of their current work. In addition to consolidating knowledge of number and calculation,

measures, geometry and data handling, they can be used as opportunities to provide variety and context. You might discuss with children observations about a mathematically-rich object, or solve a mathematical problem that has come up in the class, in the school, in the news, at home or in a story.

You can refer to the whole-class practice activities from the activity groups in the Teaching Resource Handbook for ideas. You could also select focus activities from the activity groups to use for class investigations or problem solving.

Children's mathematical thinking and reasoning can also be encouraged at other times during the day. Along with the 'morning maths meeting', this will help to ensure that they experience the full breadth of the maths curriculum, and that they do not see mathematics as something that only happens in their mathematics lessons.

The daily or weekly timetable and the school year provide a meaningful context for children to make predictions and to develop language for temporal relationships (such as 'next', 'before', 'after', 'in between' – note these terms are also used to describe the order of numbers) and for units of time (including the names of the days of the week and months of the year). Calendars, clocks, timers and stopwatches can be used to reinforce the idea of the order and passage of units of time – you might, for example, set an alarm clock or timer at the start of a particular lesson or activity, to ring at the end.

Mathematical thinking can be encouraged in a broad range of classroom tasks and activities. For example, if children are lining up you could ask them to do so in order of height or by birth month, when they are moving between places in the room or school you could ask them to estimate then measure the distance, in steps, or to describe the turns they need to take along the way.

What might the use of Numicon look like in my classroom?

Nearly all of us are acutely visually aware, and children are no exception. A mathematics-rich environment provides valuable learning opportunities; throughout the day, and particularly during mathematics activities, you will find children referring to the imagery and displays around them.

Number images and numerals can be incorporated into labels, notices and displays throughout the classroom, as well as being provided in the form of more specifically mathematical resources – number lines at children's eye level, for example.

You can also create displays to reflect children's current mathematical focus. As well as providing a space in which to celebrate children's mathematical work, this might include pictures, books, interesting objects (different types and designs of clocks, watches or timers, for instance, when children are learning about measuring or telling time) and relevant games and challenges (estimating how many repetitions of a particular skill they can complete in 30 seconds, for example, then finding out and comparing this with their actual result).

Alongside creating a visually-rich environment in which to think and communicate about mathematics, the organization of space and resources can encourage children's involvement in doing mathematics. For example,

it is useful to set up a mathematics table with an interactive display where children can freely explore Numicon Shapes, number rods, 2D and 3D shapes, measuring instruments and other familiar resources. When children are studying geometry and measurement, it is often also helpful to set up some classroom, play or outdoor space so that they can try out the equipment and practise the activities they meet in their mathematics lessons. For example, while working on capacity children might be given access to water or sand and a variety of containers; for position, direction and movement a maze could be marked on the floor using masking tape or a play-equipment obstacle course set up for children to negotiate by giving each other instructions.

Organizing classroom resources systematically, with storage containers numbered and stored in a logical order, ensures that mathematics equipment will be easily accessible for children to find and use themselves. They should be familiar with what is available to them, and encouraged to use it freely. The 'morning maths meeting' might be used, early in the year, to explore resources and how they can be used. This is also an aspect of creating a mathematics-rich environment, with the sorting and reasoning skills involved in putting away and finding resources contributing to children's mathematical thinking and communicating. Finally, geometry and measurement activities typically lend themselves to collaborative working, and some will require a suitable space to be set up in advance. As part of your preparations for a new activity group, you may wish to consider how working spaces or desks should be arranged to facilitate this. (See also 'How will I manage the class for mathematics lessons?' on page 29 and 'What about organizing resources and space?' on page 29).

What could using Numicon feel like for children in my class?

The activities in Geometry, Measurement and Statistics 1 are designed to make practical sense to children – they are introduced to coins in the context of trade and exchange, for example, and investigate real-life objects and packaging as a way of thinking about different types of 3D shapes. In this way, children are encouraged to recognize that mathematics is an ordinary, valuable and interesting part of everyday life, and of their ongoing learning about the world. As you engage them in solving mathematical problems, they also learn *when* to use mathematics.

Within the mathematics-rich environment of the classroom, you are likely to notice children glancing at displays and images to check an idea they are explaining. At other times, you will notice them simply looking thoughtfully at displays – they are likely to be noticing relationships and making connections as they assimilate new ideas.

The open-ended nature of the Numicon resources and activities invites children to experiment and explore, self-correcting as they seek solutions. Children begin to recognize self-correcting as part of the learning process; encouraging them to pursue opportunities to investigate, think, communicate and self-correct will increase their confidence.

Working in pairs within groups also supports children's confidence by encouraging them to share ideas and work things out together. Some children are more confident when working with a partner, setting challenges and exploring ideas more deeply than they do when working alone.

Children take their lead for listening to each other and sharing ideas from the ways in which the adults in the classroom converse with them and each other. They will need help with taking turns, showing respect for each other's ideas, listening to one another without interrupting, phrasing questions and expressing ideas. Over time, you will find that children become confident in sharing their thinking.

With Numicon, children will also know that there is nothing wrong with challenge: it is normal to get 'stuck' – what is important is continuing to communicate mathematically. Children come to relish challenge because they feel able to persist in the face of it, and gain a sense of achievement when a challenge is overcome. Part of this confidence comes from the ways in which their understanding is built cumulatively by following the suggested progression of teaching activities in the Teaching Resource Handbook.

Children also feel confident when tackling new ideas because they can use a variety of resources and imagery to illustrate problems. Their confidence will be further encouraged as you discuss their ideas with them, helping them to become increasingly aware of what they know and are learning. This discussion supports children's monitoring of their own learning.

What is the role of imagery in geometry and measurement?

In their work on number, children are asked from a very early point to 'handle' abstract objects, in the form of pure numbers. Numicon's focus on the use of structured materials helps them to approach this apparently contradictory task through actions and imagery, and in this way to gain access to the ideas we symbolize with numerals such as '3' or '10' (for more discussion, see the 'What is Numicon?' section).

In contrast, children's work on geometry and measurement is rooted in physical objects and how they occupy physical space – their shape, length, mass and so on. They are able to handle these objects directly and immediately: to look at the use of space around them; to draw or make, change, dismantle and remake shapes for themselves; to compare and judge size and quantity in concrete terms – according to how much of something they can fit in their own hand, for example.

Just as for number, though, learning about geometry and measurement requires children to identify relationships and develop symbolic representations (words and symbols) which enable them to spot patterns (generalize) – that is, to think and communicate mathematically. To identify any triangle successfully, for example, children must link the word 'triangle' with a generalized set of requirements which can apply in an infinite number of cases; that is, they must be able to distinguish any particular instance of a closed 2D shape with three straight sides. They can then refine their symbolic representation to identify other general types of triangle: scalene, isosceles, equilateral, right-angled, and so on.

For measurement, the reasoning is perhaps more straightforward, but the principles are the same. Identifying which measurement and unit to use requires a generalized understanding of dimensions of length (for instance), and relative sizes.

Children should be encouraged to experience and explore physical space and objects, investigating, constructing and transforming with a variety of resources and materials in a variety of contexts – but in doing this it is the dynamic mental imagery that they build up, rather than the 'raw' number of examples they encounter, that will enable them to generalize and think mathematically. It is important to support the development of children's imagery by encouraging a continual emphasis on visualizing, describing and predicting results in their work.

How much time should I plan to spend on mathematics teaching?

The time spent teaching mathematics during the school day can vary. In addition to a daily mathematics lesson lasting up to an hour and a 'morning maths meeting' lasting about 15 minutes, there are many opportunities for developing language of, e.g. comparing, position, movement, time and shape. There will also be many opportunities for estimating or making measurements as well as calculating. Taking advantage of these opportunities helps children realize that doing mathematics is normal and useful in all sorts of situations, and encourages them to recognize when and how to use the mathematics they have learned.

For planning teaching time, see the section 'How do I plan in the medium- and long-term using the Geometry, Measurement and Statistics 1 teaching programme?' on page 32.

What format might Numicon mathematics lessons take?

Look at the relevant pages of the Teaching Resource Handbook for the activity group you are working from. The first part of the mathematics lesson is a whole-class introduction. This is followed by a longer session of group work during which children are either working independently or as part of a focused teaching group. Finally, the class comes together for a concluding session.

During the lesson introduction, you are likely to use physical materials and other imagery in communicating and discussing ideas with children.

Children may join in this whole-class part of the lesson in lots of different ways: participating in a class conversation, talking with a partner or within a small group, jotting on an individual whiteboard, or using physical resources to explore and show ideas.

In the second part of the lesson, children will be arranged in groups working on, for example:

- a teacher-led focus activity
- a teaching assistant-led focus activity
- an independent practice activity or investigation, or further work on ideas introduced at the start of the lesson.

Groups will be exploring ideas within the same activity group but may not be working on the same activities. They may be using different apparatus – for example, for a lesson on length, some groups may be using lengths of string and others strips of paper, while others may be writing and drawing to record particular lengths.

Over the course of a week, the different groups may rotate through the various group-work activities, so that all children receive focus teaching, and explore the ideas using different imagery.

In the final part of the lesson, it is particularly important to encourage all children to reflect on their learning by asking questions of those working at different levels, depending on what you have noticed them doing and saying during the lesson. You may decide to ask the different groups to explain to the rest of the class what they have been doing and what they have noticed. You may have particular points you want to draw to children's attention. You could also suggest what might happen in the next lesson and anything children could think about before then. To help children reflect, you could ask them to think quietly for a few moments about what they have been doing, and guide their reflection with questions such as:

- Is there anything new you have learned?
- Is there anything you feel particularly pleased about?
- Is there anything you particularly enjoyed?
- Is there anything you found difficult?
- Is there anything you are still puzzling about?
- Is there anything you would like to do again?

How will I manage the class for mathematics lessons?

There are several important factors to consider for organizing and managing successful group work.

Firstly to engage children, it is important to plan differentiated activities that will provide appropriate levels of challenge for all children. Therefore, during the week, the group-work activities will need to be adjusted for different groups.

Secondly as children may be working on activities that have been adjusted, it is important that they are comfortable with how to do the activity and what is expected of them.

Thirdly the order in which the activities are introduced to different groups has an impact on how quickly children progress.

At the beginning of the week, the class may be taking in a lot of information, so give consideration to how you will introduce the activities, as this will impact on how quickly children can access and begin to make progress in the work. You will find ways that work well for you, but the following guidance may be of help:

- Explain the simplest independent work first.
- The first time you introduce a challenging practice activity, allocate it to a group of children who are able to follow instructions well.
- Groups which might need more support should begin the week with a focus activity; the adult working with the group can explain the activity, removing the need to spend time explaining it to the whole class.

Once the activities have been introduced, children will then go off to work in their groups. You may wish to focus on the one or two groups that need the most support at this point. If you have a teaching assistant, you may want them to work closely with the group who need the greatest assistance. Each class, and each lesson, will be different.

During this part of the lesson, it is quite likely that a child or children will put forward an idea that is worth everybody considering. You might choose to invite all children to take a moment to reflect on the idea, or make a note to discuss this in the final part of the lesson, when the class comes back together.

What about organizing resources and space?

The way in which resources are organized, used and presented and how the available space is set up sends children a strong message about how they are expected to work. (See also 'What might the use of Numicon look like in my classroom?' on page 25.)

When preparing the classroom for a mathematics lesson, consider how children will be grouped and how working spaces and desks should be arranged for particular activities and learning requirements. Set out the equipment where children are going to be working. Refer to the 'Have ready' sections of the activities you plan to teach. The photocopy masters needed can be printed from the *Geometry, Measurement and Statistics 1 Planning and Assessment Support* or photocopied from the Teaching Resource Handbook.

A number of activities in Geometry, Measurement and Statistics 1 require some open space (for example for pretend river crossings in Measurement 1, for practising a variety of skills for given lengths of time in Measurement 3, for working with water (or perhaps sand) in Measurement 5, and for an obstacle course, a maze and a short journey in Geometry 5). Again, refer to the '**Have ready**' sections of the activities in order to arrange for suitable space in advance.

It is also useful to consider collecting well in advance the real-life examples – both images and objects – which will be needed or provide context for children's work. These might include: items for sale; food items in packets, boxes and tins; patterned designs; a variety of containers; objects which are, or are made up of, common 3D shapes; and different types and designs of clock.

If you have planned for groups to take turns to do the activities over a week, it can be helpful to store the equipment for each activity in a separate container so it is ready for use each day. Encourage children to leave the resources as they found them, ready for the next group. Children can help themselves to any further equipment they need from the class mathematics resources. As children become used to working with Numicon and other mathematics apparatus, they can begin to collect the equipment they need for an activity by following a list (illustrated if necessary with pictures, symbols or container numbers), and thinking for themselves about any further items they may want to use.

Other ideas for organizing resources are:

- providing smaller containers of equipment for children working individually or in pairs
- using sorting trays with separate compartments to allow children to access resources, such as numeral cards or pattern blocks, to save space and keep the resources organized
- storing paper resources which children may want to use, such as number lines and geo strips, by hanging them from hooks (punch a hole in the end, if necessary).

What writing or drawing might children do in mathematics if the activities are mainly practical?

Writing and drawing are aspects of communicating mathematically, and children's chosen forms of this communication may be varied and idiosyncratic. They might involve: drawing a measurement in pictures – for example the number of 'weights', e.g. pencils, equal to a particular mass, arranged in Numicon Shape patterns next to the object weighed; drawing a number story in pictures or by drawing around Numicon Shapes; drawing repeating patterns; or showing sorting of objects or shapes by making all those of a particular type the same colour.

Giving children the choice of how to communicate their ideas can therefore provide useful insights into how they are approaching problems, whether they are working systematically and how they are using conventional notation. It also helps children to formulate, clarify and develop their thinking, and to think of writing and drawing as part of doing mathematics (rather than in themselves *being* mathematics).

Accordingly, opportunities for children to communicate on paper are highlighted in the activities wherever this serves

a useful purpose. Some activity sheets are provided as photocopy masters, but in general it is recommended that children write and draw in their maths exercise books. This creates a useful bank of evidence to show how children's mathematical communicating develops over time.

The Explorer Progress Book (see page 10) also provides an extremely useful source of evidence for children's progress.

What about grouping children?

Children work well in pairs within larger groups of four or six. Working with a partner supports their confidence, giving them plenty of opportunities to discuss their work and solve problems together.

Schools vary in their criteria for grouping children. When grouping children of five and six years old, it is important to bear in mind that they will be at very different levels of development and will therefore require different levels of challenge. Some schools find an advantage in having mixed-ability groups comprising pairs of children working at slightly different levels; others group together children who are working at a similar level.

Whatever the policy is in your school, bear in mind that it is important to vary groups from time to time and to ensure that children do not always work with the same partner. Some children will work faster than others and have more developed ideas. It is important to make sure that they have opportunities to work with other children of similar ability. As you follow the suggested teaching programme for the first few weeks of term, you will discover which children work well together and their levels of understanding.

How do I prepare for teaching mathematics lessons using Numicon?

Understanding the mathematics yourself

Before teaching an activity group, read the relevant sections from the Key mathematical ideas sections (pages 44–68) to prepare for your teaching. If you want to do more research on an area of mathematics, you may wish to consult other sources, for example Derek Haylock's *Mathematics Explained for Primary Teachers* (4th edition, 2010).

Next, consider what generalizing there is in the activity group. For example, 'Is this where children could notice that a rectangle might be either a square or an oblong?' Or, 'Is this where children notice that the size of an object doesn't tell you if it is heavy or not?'

The children will be new to this, so another way to work on generalizations is to ask, 'What patterns in the work children are doing will they have to notice in order to progress?'

When children notice things, be prepared to keep asking: 'Will that always work?' 'What if those quantities were different?' 'Would that work with a different shape?' 'Will that ever work?' 'When does that work?' 'What never works?'

Appreciating the contexts

The educational context on the introductory page for each activity group will help you to see how the ideas involved fit into the continuum of children's learning about geometry, measurement and statistics.

After reading this educational context, consider when this learning may be useful. Children don't just need to know

how to do this mathematics, they need to know *when* to do it as well. How can you help them spot when this general mathematics applies to a particular situation?

Think about the kinds of contexts offered in the activity group, and ask yourself whether the mathematics is useful in particular kinds of real-world situations, or whether it helps with doing other mathematics. It can be helpful to think up one or two contexts of your own, so that it is clear what the point of doing this mathematics is.

Selecting and adapting activities

You know the children in your class and the materials and spaces which are available to you. You will be best placed to select which activities are most appropriate and adapt them creatively to suit the needs of individual children.

Read all of the activities in an activity group and identify what each activity contributes overall, as well as the resources and preparation involved. Then try the activities. Some might be 'revision' for your children, others might involve ideas, illustrations or techniques that are completely new. Some activities will be invaluable practice. You might think an activity will be too easy or too difficult for some children, so think about how you might adjust the level of challenge. Be flexible and adapt what is available for your children in the light of what they can already do.

It's also worth considering that challenge is normal; when children get 'stuck', they should be encouraged to communicate. Make sure they have available all the actions, imagery and language they need to communicate the challenge they are facing effectively.

How do I plan in the medium- and long-term using the Geometry, Measurement and Statistics 1 teaching programme?

The plan-teach-review cycle applies to Numicon, just as it applies to all effective mathematics teaching. Four important features of Numicon support this cycle:

Firstly the Numicon teaching programme – the recommended order of the activity groups – is structured progressively. A chart showing the programme appears in the long- and medium-term planning sections of the *Geometry, Measurement and Statistics 1 Teaching Resource Handbook*; an editable version is also available in the Planning and Assessment Support.

Secondly practice and discussion activities are included in each activity group, for individual, paired and group work.

Thirdly accurate assessment is enabled through children's practical work with physical resources and imagery, and their mathematical communicating in conversation and on paper. This assessment will, in turn, help with planning.

Finally, 'using and applying' does not need to be planned separately. This is partly because all activity groups are based around problems to be solved, and partly because the cumulative nature of the programme means that children are using their earlier learning every time they face new ideas.

The teaching programme for Geometry, Measurement and Statistics 1 is arranged into two strands, Geometry and Measurement, with a series of activity groups within each. Both include some early coverage of Statistics, in the

form of simple data handling and recording in tables, and opportunities to create pictograms.

The long-term plan on page 17 of the *Geometry, Measurement and Statistics 1 Teaching Resource Handbook* shows the recommended order of the activity groups. It has been carefully designed to scaffold children's understanding, so that they are able to meet the challenges of each new idea. For example, children would not be expected to distinguish a 'clockwise' from an 'anticlockwise' turn before having recall of how a clock's hands move.

It should be noted that this structure has been designed together with the progression of the *Numicon Number, Pattern and Calculating 1* teaching programme. The long-term plan included on the *Numicon Planning and Assessment Support* contains suggestions for integrating the *Geometry, Measurement and Statistics 1* activity groups with those from the *Number, Pattern and Calculating 1 Teaching Resource Handbook*.

The medium-term plan on pages 18–22 of the *Geometry, Measurement and Statistics 1 Teaching Resource Handbook* gives expected coverage over the course of the year and also lists the activities and learning opportunities for each group.

You may decide to follow the long- and medium-term plans as they stand. You may also find that you need to split some of the larger activity groups and return to them later.

There are summary charts showing learning opportunities for each activity group in the long- and medium-term planning section of the *Geometry, Measurement and Statistics 1 Teaching Resource Handbook* and in the Planning and Assessment Support. You may find these useful for incorporating Numicon activities into your existing mathematics plans, should you decide not to follow the Numicon long-term plan for teaching the activity groups.

The parts and structure of each activity group are highlighted in the key to the activity groups on pages 8 and 9 of the Teaching Resource Handbook.

Each activity group begins with a 'low-threshold' focus activity designed to encourage and support confidence and ensure that all children are included. The remaining focus activities are designed to help children progressively develop their ideas around the mathematical theme of the activity group. The focus activities are designed for whole-class or group teaching. Some may be taught quite quickly to the whole class as an introduction to be explored later with a focus group. Opportunities for reasoning through challenging questions and problems are provided throughout.

Ensure that activities are differentiated where necessary so that all children who should be working independently can do so. Include activities that enable children to become more confident; encourage them to work more effectively and speedily through practising and celebrating what they are able to do. As you decide which activity to allocate to a particular group, remember to check that there is scope for children to take the activity further. You can increase the challenge by asking more challenging questions, either with specific groups or when the class comes together for the final part of the lesson. Your questions will depend on what you have noticed the children doing and saying as they work.

How long should I spend on each activity group?

The Numicon teaching activities for Geometry, Measurement and Statistics 1 primarily address the shape, position and measurement areas of the curriculum, along with some aspects of number.

For children who are new to Numicon, you may need to allow one or two weeks for making connections between Numicon Shapes and Shape patterns, number rods, number names and numerals. (For example, through the activities in the 'Securing Foundations' activity groups in the *Number, Pattern and Calculating 1 Teaching Resource Handbook*.)

There are 11 activity groups within the *Geometry, Measurement and Statistics 1 Teaching Resource Handbook*. Some of the activity groups contain more material than can be covered in one week: you might choose to work right through the activity group, have a break while you teach another topic, or even make selections from the activity group and integrate the material with work on other areas of mathematics. Returning to finish a group after a week or so has the advantage of reminding children about the ideas they have met previously, and gives you a useful opportunity to review what they have remembered. Alternatively, you may prefer to revisit or cover some ideas with whole-class practice at different times during the day, in particular during the 'morning maths meeting'. You will also find that children sometimes move very quickly through the work, and you will be able to combine two or sometimes three activities in one focus teaching session.

What about differentiating activities?

It is important for children of all abilities that activities provide appropriate levels of challenge.

The educational context and learning opportunities on the introductory page of each activity group give you an overview of the ideas children will meet and the learning to be built upon. If your assessments tell you that some children are not yet ready for the activity group, you can look back through earlier activity groups in the same strand to find appropriate activities. If the number content is too challenging, it may be appropriate to differentiate by, for example, adjusting the number range used in the activities; alternatively, consider whether it is best to revisit activities later, once children are more secure in the required knowledge.

Each activity group starts with a 'low-threshold' activity designed to be accessible to all children. In a mixed-age class you may need to modify the work for younger children and assess how they respond. You may decide some children are ready to go straight to more challenging activities, later in the activity group.

The open-ended nature of the activities and the emphasis on mathematical thinking means that there is always room for children to take activities further. For the highest-achieving children, you may decide to increase the challenge by planning specific questions that extend the reach of the activity. Encourage them to 'get stuck' and work through problems for themselves, by exploring and refining ways of communicating the ideas involved. You might, for example, challenge them to create their own problems for others to solve.

How can I support children to develop fluency and flexibility?

Each activity group includes suggestions for whole-class and independent practice and discussion to help children develop fluent understanding of the ideas they are meeting and to look at situations in different ways, considering a variety of approaches. You can select from these to give children appropriately differentiated opportunities that will help them to develop confidence.

The Explore More Copymasters provide further opportunities for children to practise and discuss at home the ideas they have been working on at school. The 'morning maths meeting' also provides an excellent opportunity for practice and discussion.

How can I support children to maintain fluency and flexibility?

Children's responses to questions and problems and ability to give examples or make up their own questions in the 'morning maths meeting' or other practice sessions will indicate whether they are maintaining fluency with past learning and thinking flexibly.

You might choose an activity from the practice section of a completed activity group, vary the context and present it to children without preparing them in advance – notice what they do and do not seem to remember, and plan accordingly for the next related activity group. You can also use questions and activities from previous activity groups to help keep children's past learning and creative thinking 'simmering'.

Using the activity groups

The first page of each activity group is clearly coloured according to the **strand** it appears in (Geometry – green, Measurement – purple; early statistics work is introduced within these strands through appropriate contexts). The title and the numbering of the activity group allow you to easily identify the content of the activity group and how far through the strand you are.

The **key mathematical ideas** clearly highlight the important ideas children will be meeting within each activity group.

The **assessment opportunities** signal key information to 'look and listen for' that indicate how much of the focus activities children have understood.

The **educational context** gives a clear outline of the content covered in the activity group, for example how it builds on children's prior learning; how it connects with other activity groups; the foundation it establishes for children's future learning.

All activity groups have been extensively trialled in the classroom, so the **learning opportunities** come from real classroom experiences. They are designed to help children develop their understanding of the key ideas of an activity group.

Key mathematical ideas Money, Equivalence **Measurement**

Introducing the 1p, 2p, 5p and 10p coins 2

Educational context

In this activity group children encounter the idea of how much something is 'worth' in the context of trading in markets or shops, and are introduced to money as an agreed measure of this worth. This broad introduction can be used to encourage children to recall related contexts and language from their own experience, and to begin to think about what money is. You could talk with them, for example, about buying and selling, value and price, bargaining and fairness.

The 1p and 2p, 5p and 10p coins are introduced and children make a thorough investigation of their relative values, using structured apparatus as needed to total amounts up to 20p and explore equivalences. They reason systematically to work out how to pay with the fewest coins, or to find all the possible ways of paying. Following this work, in the *Number, Pattern and Calculating 1 Teaching Resource Handbook* there are opportunities to build on this learning in areas such as number facts, equivalence, and doubling and halving (covered, for instance, in Calculating 3 and 6, and Pattern and Algebra 2).

Learning opportunities

- To consider the value and worth of given items by trading them.
- To understand buying as exchanging money for items.
- To recognize a variety of coins.
- To understand the value of 1p, 2p, 5p and 10p coins.
- To be able to make different amounts of money using one or more types of coin.

Words and terms for use in conversation

trade, swap, exchange, worth, fair, money, pence (p), coin, coins, penny, pennies, one, two, five, ten, twenty, fifty, more, less, fewer, make, spend, spent, price, cost, buy, bought, sold, sell, pay, bronze, silver

Assessment opportunities

Look and listen for children who:

- Use the words and terms for use in conversation effectively.
- Sort and identify coins correctly.
- Know the relative value of 1p, 2p, 5p and 10p coins.
- Make amounts up to 20p using a variety of coins.
- Find all possible combinations of coins for an amount from 5p to 20p.
- Give the correct amount of money up to 20p when buying an item using 1p, 2p, 5p and 10p coins.
- Make any amount of money, up to 20p, in the smallest number of coins possible.

Explorer Progress Book 1, pp. 6–7

After completing work on this activity group, give small focus groups of children their Explorer Progress Books and ask them to work through the challenges on the pages.
As children complete the pages, assess what progress they are making with the central ideas from the activity group.
Refer to the assessment opportunities for assistance.

Explore More Copymaster 7: Collecting Coins

After completing work on Activity 2, give children Explore More Copymaster 7: Collecting Coins to take home.

Explore More Copymasters provide an opportunity for children to practise the mathematics from the activity group outside the classroom through fun, engaging activities.

Clear links are made to the **Explorer Progress Book**. This book provides an invaluable chance to see children's thinking, monitor their progress and assess how much of the activity group they have understood.

Each activity group includes several **focus activities**, each clearly titled to show the specific learning points addressed by the activity. The first focus activity is a 'low threshold' activity allowing all children to engage with the work. Focus activities then build progressively to a 'high ceiling' that provides challenge and allows for differentiation within the same activity group.

The **Have ready** section at the start of each focus activity provides a clear list of the equipment that is used to help support children's learning.

Focus activities are broken down into **step-by-step** instructions.

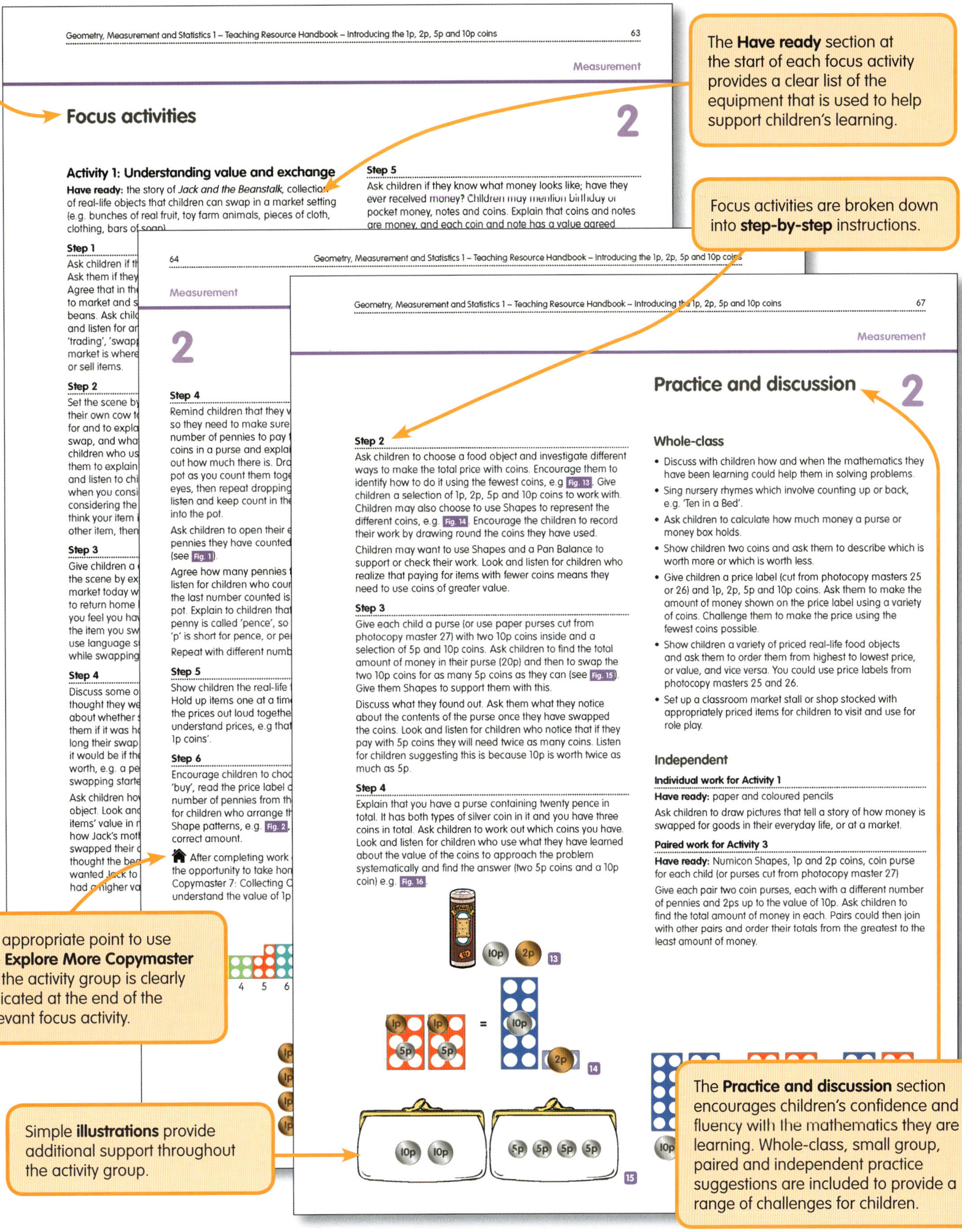

Geometry, Measurement and Statistics 1 – Teaching Resource Handbook – Introducing the 1p, 2p, 5p and 10p coins 63

Measurement

Focus activities

2

Activity 1: Understanding value and exchange

Have ready: the story of *Jack and the Beanstalk*, collection of real-life objects that children can swap in a market setting (e.g. bunches of real fruit, toy farm animals, pieces of cloth, clothing, bars of soap)

Step 5

Ask children if they know what money looks like; have they ever received money? Children may mention birthday or pocket money, notes and coins. Explain that coins and notes are money, and each coin and note has a value agreed

64 Geometry, Measurement and Statistics 1 – Teaching Resource Handbook – Introducing the 1p, 2p, 5p and 10p coins

Measurement

2

Geometry, Measurement and Statistics 1 – Teaching Resource Handbook – Introducing the 1p, 2p, 5p and 10p coins 67

Measurement

Practice and discussion

2

Step 2

Ask children to choose a food object and investigate different ways to make the total price with coins. Encourage them to identify how to do it using the fewest coins, e.g. Fig. 13. Give children a selection of 1p, 2p, 5p and 10p coins to work with. Children may also choose to use Shapes to represent the different coins, e.g. Fig. 14. Encourage the children to record their work by drawing round the coins they have used.

Children may want to use Shapes and a Pan Balance to support or check their work. Look and listen for children who realize that paying for items with fewer coins means they need to use coins of greater value.

Step 3

Give each child a purse (or use paper purses cut from photocopy master 27) with two 10p coins inside and a selection of 5p and 10p coins. Ask children to find the total amount of money in their purse (20p) and then to swap the two 10p coins for as many 5p coins as they can (see Fig. 15). Give them Shapes to support them with this.

Discuss what they found out. Ask them what they notice about the contents of the purse once they have swapped the coins. Look and listen for children who notice that if they pay with 5p coins they will need twice as many coins. Listen for children suggesting this is because 10p is worth twice as much as 5p.

Step 4

Explain that you have a purse containing twenty pence in total. It has both types of silver coin in it and you have three coins in total. Ask children to work out which coins you have. Look and listen for children who use what they have learned about the value of the coins to approach the problem systematically and find the answer (two 5p coins and a 10p coin) e.g. Fig. 16.

Whole-class

- Discuss with children how and when the mathematics they have been learning could help them in solving problems.
- Sing nursery rhymes which involve counting up or back, e.g. 'Ten in a Bed'.
- Ask children to calculate how much money a purse or money box holds.
- Show children two coins and ask them to describe which is worth more or which is worth less.
- Give children a price label (cut from photocopy masters 25 or 26) and 1p, 2p, 5p and 10p coins. Ask them to make the amount of money shown on the price label using a variety of coins. Challenge them to make the price using the fewest coins possible.
- Show children a variety of priced real-life food objects and ask them to order them from highest to lowest price, or value, and vice versa. You could use price labels from photocopy masters 25 and 26.
- Set up a classroom market stall or shop stocked with appropriately priced items for children to visit and use for role play.

Independent

Individual work for Activity 1

Have ready: paper and coloured pencils

Ask children to draw pictures that tell a story of how money is swapped for goods in their everyday life, or at a market.

Paired work for Activity 3

Have ready: Numicon Shapes, 1p and 2p coins, coin purse for each child (or purses cut from photocopy master 27)

Give each pair two coin purses, each with a different number of pennies and 2ps up to the value of 10p. Ask children to find the total amount of money in each. Pairs could then join with other pairs and order their totals from the greatest to the least amount of money.

An appropriate point to use the **Explore More Copymaster** for the activity group is clearly indicated at the end of the relevant focus activity.

Simple **illustrations** provide additional support throughout the activity group.

The **Practice and discussion** section encourages children's confidence and fluency with the mathematics they are learning. Whole-class, small group, paired and independent practice suggestions are included to provide a range of challenges for children.

Planning and assessment cycle

This summary shows how planning is informed by your assessments of children's understanding:

1. Choose an activity group	Before embarking on the activity group, review the educational context, consider your initial assessments of children and decide whether there is a need to revise any ideas children have met earlier.
2. Choose a focus activity	If this is the first lesson using the activity group, start with an early 'low-threshold' activity to include all children. Before the lesson, check the learning and assessment opportunities, brief teaching assistants and prepare resources.
3. Choose the practice activities	**Independent groups:** Refer to your assessment notes and allocate suitable practice activities (found at the end of the activity group). **Focus teaching groups:** Refer to your assessment notes and the learning and assessment opportunities from the activity group and allocate focus activities.
4. Plenary session (normally during and at the end of lessons)	Think about the important ideas that children meet in the lesson, particularly any generalizations that you want children to make. Plan questions to prompt discussion and encourage children to reflect on ideas they may have learned. Refer to the practice section of the activity group to find suggestions for whole-class practice.
5. After the lesson	Reflect on how children have responded in the lesson and note any significant steps on your assessment records. Use what you notice to determine the plan for the next lesson. The whole-class practice suggestions will also help children develop the ideas they have learned in the lesson. At some point after children have completed the activity group, ask them to complete the relevant pages of their Explorer Progress Book. This will allow you to assess how well they have retained the information they have been learning. It will also give you a chance to see how well they are able to apply this knowledge when faced with a 'non-routine' problem.

Creating short-term plans

	Warm-up	Main teaching focus	Focused group work with the class teacher or teaching assistant	Independent work	Plenary
Activity number/title	Select activities from the **Whole-class practice** section. This could be from a previous activity group to review and refresh children's previous learning.	Select one of the focus activities from the activity group, matched to the needs of the children. Place the **activity number/title** of the chosen focus activity in your short-term plan.	Decide whether to: • select the next **activity number/ title** from the focus activities in the activity group. Place this in your short-term plan; or • consolidate the activity covered in the main teaching focus.	Decide whether to: • choose activities from the **Independent practice** section for groups, pairs or individual children. Make notes on your plan or work from the Teaching Resource Handbook; or • select a focus activity for groups to work on independently. Place the relevant **activity number/ title** in your short-term plan.	Encourage children to have a reflective conversation to draw together what has been learned in the lesson. Select activities from the **Whole-class practice** section.
Learning opportunities	Place the selected learning opportunities, from the chosen activity group summary in your short-term plan.				
Notes and educational context	Decide whether to: • use the activity directly from your Numicon *Geometry, Measurement and Statistics 1 Teaching Resource Handbook*; or • draw on the Teaching Resource Handbook to make your own notes for teaching the activity.	Decide whether to: • use the focus activity from your Numicon *Geometry, Measurement and Statistics 1 Teaching Resource Handbook*; or • draw on the Teaching Resource Handbook to make your own notes for teaching the focus activity.	Decide whether to: • use the focus activity from your Numicon *Geometry, Measurement and Statistics 1 Teaching Resource Handbook*; or • draw on the Teaching Resource Handbook to make your own notes for teaching the focus activity. If working with a teaching assistant, you may want to select the relevant **Educational context**, from the chosen activity group.	Decide whether to: • use the practice or focus activity from your Numicon *Geometry, Measurement and Statistics 1 Teaching Resource Handbook*; or • draw on the Teaching Resource Handbook to make your own notes for teaching the focus activity.	
Words and terms	Decide which **words and terms** you will use in **conversation**. Place these in your short-term plan.				
Resources	Prepare any resources you may need for the activity. Use the **have ready** section at the beginning of the focus and practice activities.				
Assessment opportunities	Select from the chosen activity group summary the **assessment opportunities** that you and the teaching assistant will be looking and listening for in the different parts of the lesson. Place these in your short-term plan. Remember to note whether children know when to use their understanding.				

How can I assess children's progress?

Assessing mathematics using Numicon involves making judgements about developments in children's mathematical communicating – both receptive and expressive. You need to know which are the key developments to look for: check the assessment opportunities given on the introductory page of each activity group and consider how the achievements listed would show up in children's mathematical communicating. Look for developments in children's actions (what they do and notice), the imagery they use and respond to, and listen for their use of and responses to words and symbols in their conversation.

It is also important to notice children's fluency; when their communicating is stilted, when it is punctuated by gaps and hesitations, and when it flows consistently and well, suggesting a strong understanding of well-established ideas and the connections between them.

Assessment should be as open as possible so that children can communicate as much as possible. It is through their mathematical communicating that you will gain a real insight into how children are thinking. This will enable you to make the most accurate assessment of their progress.

Specific challenges for the purposes of assessing are provided in the form of the Explorer Progress Book (see page 10). Children cannot pass or fail these assessment tasks – they simply respond in their own way. How they approach the tasks informs you about their mathematical communicating and gives you an opportunity to 'see' their thinking through the imagery they use. This insight makes it easier to gather meaningful and accurate evidence of where children are. Preparing for formal test situations is something different, and is addressed on page 42.

Specific indications of children's progress

Each activity group lists several assessment opportunities that point to key achievements to look and listen for as children work on the activities. All of these achievements will be observable in children's actions, imagery and conversation as they progress.

Familiarize yourself with the assessment opportunities before you begin teaching an activity group. Use them to help guide your interactions with children, and also as indicators of progress and sources of information to help you group children and plan your teaching as you move on to further activity groups.

Suggestions for what to 'look and listen' for are given within each activity. Focus on children's communicating and ask yourself whether they know both how to do the mathematics they are learning and when to use it.

You will also find that how children use physical resources gives an insight into their thinking. If a child is using pattern blocks or weights by trial and error and giving a muddled explanation, this would suggest they don't yet understand the activity. Plan to revisit it, focusing on careful use of mathematical language and imagery as well as their actions.

Children self-correcting – that is, working by trial and improvement rather than simply by trial and error – suggests their understanding is developing. Give them time to experiment and practise the activity and encourage them to discuss their ideas.

Children communicating clearly about what they have done, whether with apparatus, in conversation or on paper, suggests they have gained a solid understanding. Plan, then, to move them on.

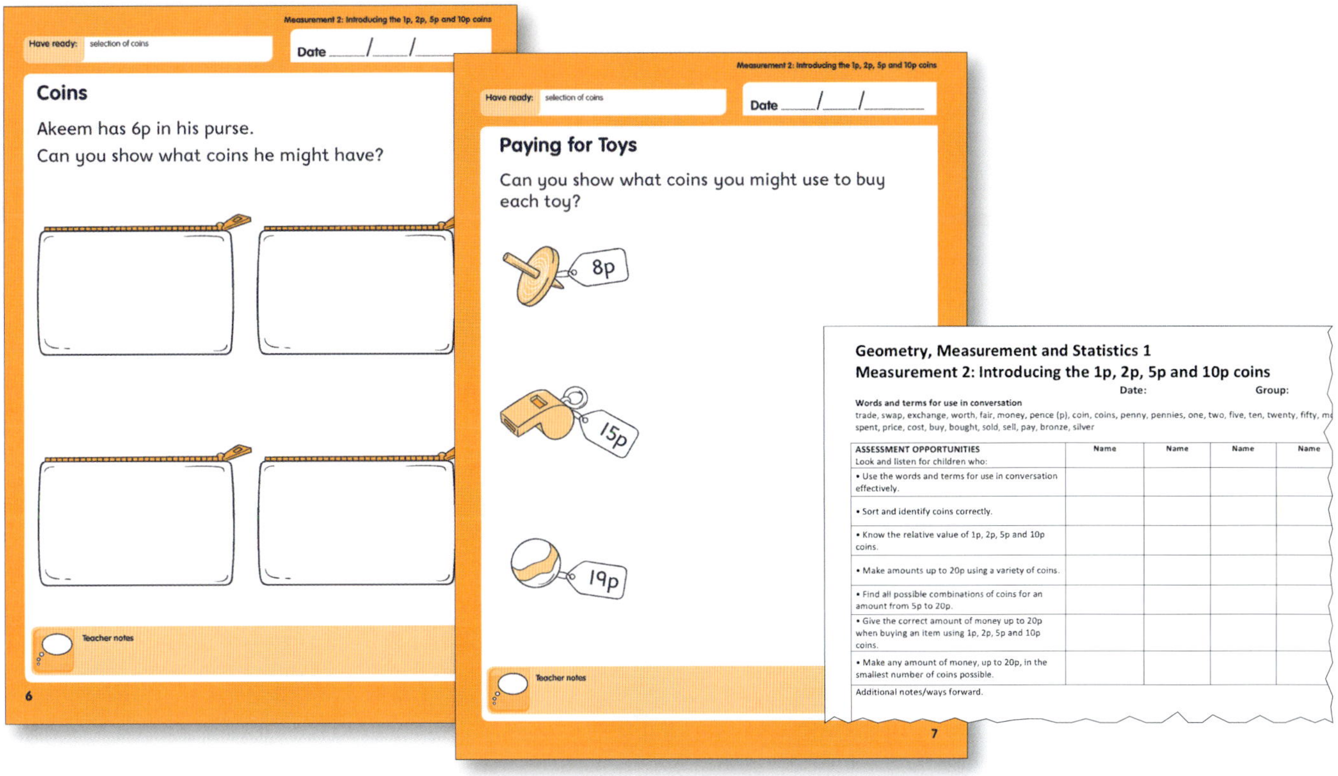

What about summative assessing?

Assessment milestones and tracking children's progress

The medium-term plan in the *Geometry, Measurement and Statistics 1 Teaching Resource Handbook* includes milestones – summary statements of specific points that children need to have a good understanding of before they move on to the next set of activity groups.

The milestones are based on the assessment opportunities in the preceding activity groups and are also aligned to the national curriculum in England (2014). Your ongoing assessment of each child will build up over the preceding period and you can keep a record of attainment and track progress using the photocopy master of the milestones for the year on pages 95 and 96 of the Teaching Resource Handbook.

Each milestone represents a point at which to reflect on each child's achievement and decide whether you need to plan further support and practice for them, giving them time to consolidate their understanding, or whether they are ready to move on. If children are moved on before they are ready their difficulties are likely to be compounded, because they will not be adequately prepared for the new ideas they meet.

Explorer Progress Book

Each activity group has two corresponding pages in the Explorer Progress Book. The first page presents children with opportunities to use the mathematics they have been learning in the activity group. The second provides more open tasks, allowing children to further apply their learning.

The Explorer Progress Book is designed to be tackled in focus groups, so that you can administer and monitor each child's responses. In this way, you are able to build up a cumulative idea of a child's progress. The tasks enable you to assess children's ability to think mathematically and persist in their work, as well as whether they understand when to use particular mathematics techniques. They are as open as possible, inviting a full range of responses. They are not pass or fail tests, rather they are there to support you in assessing as accurately as possible children's current understanding, so that you know what needs addressing. It may be useful to keep notes on children's responses and what you see as their significance for future work.

Consider carefully when to give children each Explorer Progress Book task. You might ask them to complete one page at the end of their work on the activity group and then the other two weeks later, to check how much they may have retained. Alternatively, you might give children both pages after they have completed the next activity group, or just before they face the next related activity group. The aim is to gather information about children's understanding at a point when this information is useful for their learning – decide which is the most useful point, in each case.

Children should have available to them all the materials and imagery that have been available during the teaching of the activity group, and should be invited to express what they are doing as they do it. It is best to avoid affirming or denying anything a child says or does as they work. Look and listen for what children can do without your guidance.

What about formal testing for national authorities?

Formal tests and examinations are important hurdles for children and teachers, parents and carers, schools, universities, professionals, employers and governments. They also tend to be artificial settings in which to 'do' mathematics. In this sense a formal test does not correspond to children's encounters with mathematics in their learning or everyday lives, and this means devoting time to preparing them for the uniqueness of the experience.

In a formal mathematics test, communicating is almost always restricted to 'on-paper' forms; this allows for some imagery, but not usually for action with physical materials. Also, the language used in test papers can be very formal. Thus children will need plenty of practice at interpreting such language and 'internalizing' their use of action and imagery. The development of mental imagery is a key aspect of Numicon, and children should be encouraged to 'imagine' actions, objects, movements and shapes as often as possible.

Children will also need to prepare for encountering 'difficulty' during formal tests. In their mathematics lessons, they are encouraged to express difficulty – to explain why something is challenging and to use action and imagery to illustrate their thinking. Under exam conditions they will need to respond positively to being 'stuck' by communicating mathematically with themselves, working silently to express what the trouble is and using mental imagery to explore possible solutions.

Tests and examinations should not become the paradigm for 'doing mathematics', however. Children need to learn to function mathematically in a very wide range of situations. For ongoing assessment of children's understanding, allow them the full range of actions, imagery and conversation, and encourage them to communicate mathematically in their own ways.

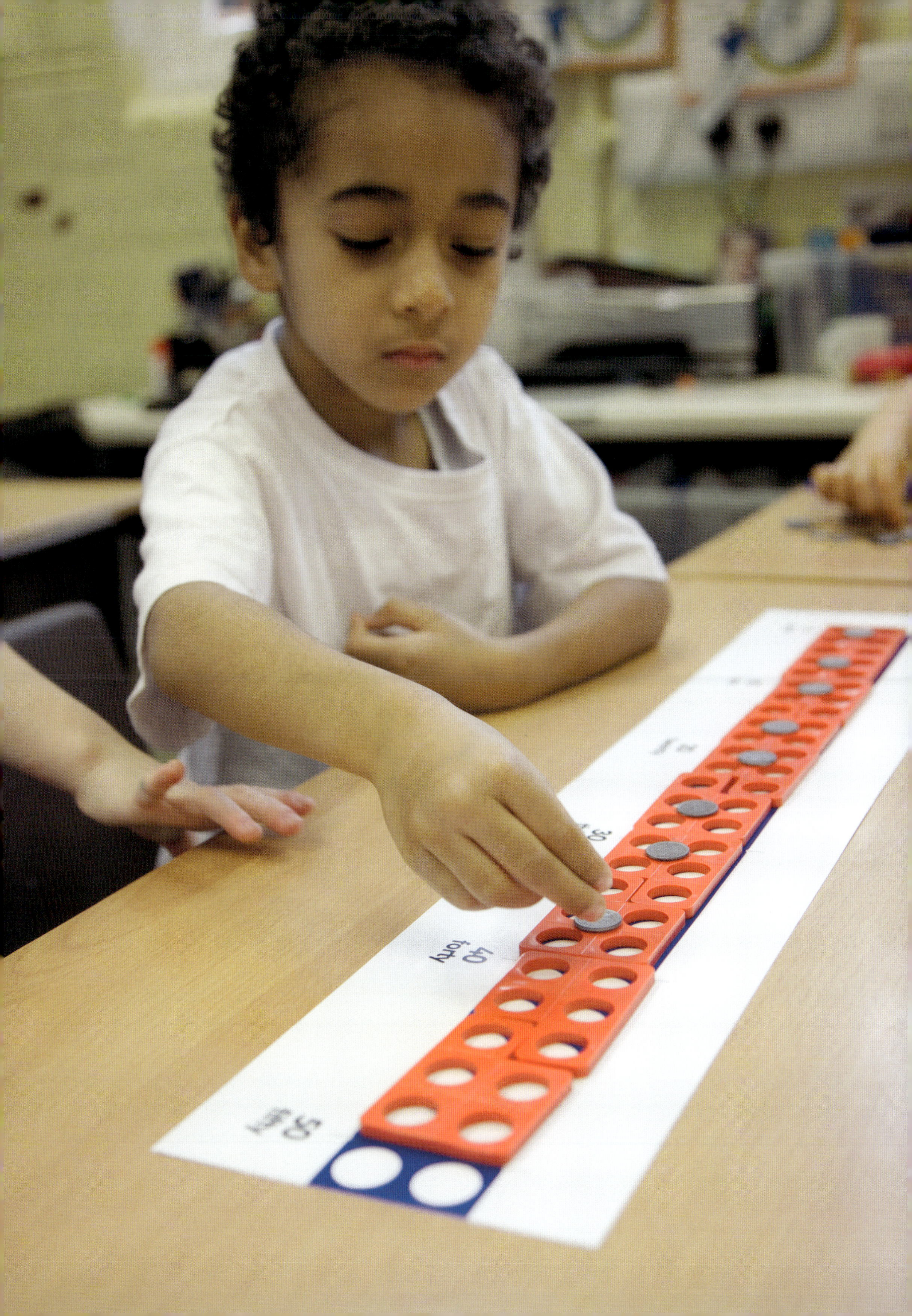

30
40
forty
50

Key mathematical ideas: Geometry in the primary years

Underlying the activities in Geometry, Measurement and Statistics 1 are many key mathematical ideas that children will be developing and extending, as well as some conventions they may be meeting for the first time.

In order to teach these ideas effectively, those who are working on the activities with children will need to be clear themselves about the mathematical ideas and about which activities address which ideas.

The following section includes a brief outline of the key mathematical ideas that children will be encountering in the Geometry activity groups of the *Geometry, Measurement and Statistics 1 Teaching Resource Handbook*. The introductory page for each activity group lists the key mathematical ideas associated with each activity. As you prepare for your teaching, you may find it helpful to remind yourself about the key ideas behind each activity by referring to this section.

The mathematics coordinator may also find it useful to work on the key mathematical ideas in professional development sessions with the class teachers and the wider school staff.

Introduction

It is important to remember that doing geometry, measurement, and using statistics are significantly related aspects of mathematics, and that each of these areas of activity has strong connections with the other two. It is important to remember too that all three also have strong connections with number, pattern, and calculating activity.

'Geometry' in ancient Greek means 'earth measurement'; many physical measures involve geometrical ideas (e.g. pressure is usually measured per 'square' unit), and patterns in data (themselves usually records of measuring activity) are commonly represented visually – as are numbers themselves, of course, in the form of number lines.

Each of these areas of mathematical activity also has its own distinctive concerns: shapes are commonly classified with little reference to their size; we measure time, force, and temperature as well as distance, area, and volume, and in statistics we are often concerned to interpret and illustrate a 'significance' in identified relationships. In what follows we treat these three broad areas of mathematical activity relatively separately for ease of reference to their key ideas, but when you are teaching each area be sure to exploit inter-connections at every opportunity.

Geometry in the primary years

Children begin exploring shape and space literally as soon as they are born. In fact it was Piaget's view that young children's first experiences of the physical world are closely related to the central ideas of a relatively recent geometry called topology. (In topology, key ideas include 'proximity', 'enclosure', and 'inter-connectedness', and it is easy to understand why such things are so important to infants from their earliest days[1].)

In order to engage children in doing geometry at school, they need first-hand experiences with shapes and with position, direction, and movement, within which shared opportunities arise both to describe actions, movements and observations freely and to introduce conventional mathematical names and terms. The point of using mathematically conventional language is to help develop 'a common way of seeing' a world with children, a common way of *communicating* about a geometrical world, so that we can share our individual perceptions and experiences with each other more easily. In the early years, children spend much of their time learning to join in with established geometrical conventions (ways of seeing and describing), as well as developing their individual 'seeing eye'; these two aspects need to proceed together, in close relation to each other.

The importance of first-hand practical experiences for children is two-fold: young children do not yet think about shape and space in the same ways that adults do, and for communicating to become effective in any context there

1 If you want an example of topology in adult use, think about a map of the London Underground and about why such ideas are the important ones in this context.

has to be a shared underlying experience that all involved can build their communicating upon. (It is very difficult to communicate effectively about, say, a film that only one of you has seen; similarly, it is very difficult to *discuss* with children things that only you have experienced). Children should be physically active and thoughtfully reflective in their geometry activities, and fully involved in *discussion* in all activities. It is only children's *agreement* to join in with doing mathematics and its established social conventions that will open up its possibilities to them; children asked to use terms they can't relate to their personal experience – however important we might think those terms are – will find themselves easily forgetting those words.

Bear in mind also that in learning to do geometry in school, children are encountering some very old conventions traditionally used in classifying 'shapes' and describing 'position', the origins of which often lie quite literally thousands of years ago. It is quite easy for children sometimes to feel that they have to learn a strange foreign language to talk about abstract shapes in school, the point of which (at the time) can seem obscure. As with medicine and the law though, many of the terms we use today in geometry have Greek and/or Latin origins and make good descriptive sense in those ancient languages, e.g. 'tri-angle' meaning three angles. Today, using words like 'polygon' and 'quadrilateral' can seem a bit odd and rather fussy, but if children are introduced to the Latin and Greek roots of these terms (e.g. 'poly' meaning 'many', and 'quad' meaning 'four') they quickly get used to connecting the sense of these old words with what they are used to describe, and this deeper level of reading can help develop their geometrical thinking and communicating significantly.

Doing geometry – transformations, invariants and equivalence

An important general point concerns the history of geometry and consequently what we tend to emphasize today in schooling. For many hundreds of years after the Greeks and Romans there was effectively only one kind of geometry used in western civilization – that of Euclid (fl. 300 BCE). But during the 19th century CE, mathematicians' attention began to focus on connecting new and ever more varied kinds of geometry with each other.

One key connecting idea turned out to be no longer thinking of geometry as simply 'earth measurement', but instead as the study of 'invariants under transformations': people began to think of geometry as studying what changes, and what stays the same, as various transformations (e.g. 'rotating', 'reflecting' or 'translating') are performed on shapes and space.

With the introduction of this idea, Euclid's traditional geometry has today become a concern with studying what stays the same (invariant) as we transform shapes. For example, a square will still have equal sides and four right-angles, equal diagonals, the same area and so on, however it is rotated, reflected, or moved about. Whereas topology is concerned with what stays the same under what are called 'rubber-sheet' transformations – imagine what happens to shapes drawn on a rubber sheet as the sheet is pulled and stretched in any ways that you like; a 'square' when stretched about on rubber will still form a continuous boundary (thus keep an 'inside' and an 'outside') so we would say that 'enclosure' is invariant, and points that are close together originally will stay relatively close together, so we say that 'proximity' is also an invariant under topological transformations. Actual

measured distances and angles all change when shapes are stretched and pulled, and so they are not invariants.

Those topological invariants are the only ones that matter to a traveller on an underground system, and also in young infants' spatial worlds. Studying 'invariants' under different kinds of transformations turns out to be a very useful way of understanding shape and space, and this informs children's geometrical activity in school today: essentially we want children to *explore* 'What happens if we *do* this ...?'

This in itself requires a necessarily *active* approach to doing geometry. We want children to be dynamically making shapes, and moving shapes (and themselves), and noticing and discussing what changes and what stays the same. 'Transforming' involves action, as does moving between and among 'positions', and *discussing* all this action is what allows children gradually to join in with the language and conventions of doing the geometry that we use in mathematics today. Gradually too, children will begin to learn how we *reason* about aspects of shapes and space in doing mathematics.

Equivalence

Just as children need to learn about equivalence in number work and algebra (e.g. $2 \times 3 = 6$, and $a + b = b + a$), so they will meet important equivalence relations in geometry. In primary school geometry, equivalence judgements are typically made in relation to specified transformations. Most commonly, children will learn that two shapes are 'the same as' each other if they could be rotated, reflected, and/or translated onto each other; two such shapes are called **congruent** to each other. If two shapes could be rotated, reflected, translated, and/or *scaled up or down* onto each other they are said to be **similar**.

Importantly, transformations can be performed one after the other, and some sequences of transformations are *equivalent* to each other in that shapes 'end up in the same state/place' after them. For example, a rotation of 180° about a point, followed by another rotation of 180° about that point, is *equivalent to* one single rotation of 360° about the point. Investigating sequences of transformations and their equivalences explicitly is a significant part of school geometry, though children will have already begun to explore this in their very early pre-school play with their simple handling of shapes (e.g. fitting different shapes into differently-shaped holes).

Doing geometry – being logical

As in doing any kind of mathematics, when we do geometry we reason by making and using **generalizations**. Indeed, this is one key aspect that distinguishes doing geometry from measuring; when we measure, we are always measuring something specific, something particular.

Being logical in doing mathematics usually involves using what is called deductive logic[2]; and *deducing* something involves moving from a general statement to a particular one. For example, knowing that 'the exterior angles of any polygon add up to 360°' allows us to deduce that the exterior angles of a triangle will add up to 360° because a triangle is a polygon. By using generalizations in various logical ways in mathematics, we can be sure that our reasoning is reliable.

2 There is a form of reasoning used in mathematics called 'proof by induction' because it moves from particular relations to a general conclusion about a whole sequence of relations. This form of proof nevertheless also relies upon at least one initial generalization about the sequence involved, for its validity.

As another example, we know that we could not try to tile a flat surface with regular pentagonal tiles because each interior angle of a regular pentagon is 108°, and there is no way you can fit a whole number of 108° angles together to make a 360° complete intersection (that is, leaving no gaps), because 360 ÷ 108 = 3·33, which is not a whole number. This is a **logical** argument: if the exterior angles of a regular pentagon add up to 360° (because it also is a polygon), then each exterior angle must be 72° (because 360 ÷ 5 = 72). If each exterior angle is 72°, then each interior angle must be 108° (because an interior and an exterior angle added together make a straight line, that is, 180°, and 180 – 72 = 108).

We have no choice about accepting reasoning like this; if our generalizations are valid our conclusion is *necessarily* correct. Notice in the preceding paragraph just how much this reasoning depends upon using our *generalizations* (including numbers themselves), *logic* and ***definitions*** (e.g. of exterior angles). Doing geometry, that is, reasoning about shape and space relationships, depends crucially upon such logic, our definitions and generalizations.

It is worth noting too, that though we may make, move and draw physical shapes on paper to help us to think, our logical reasoning is about shapes *in general*. Importantly, we can only contemplate such general shapes in our heads, that is, we can draw a particular triangle of particular dimensions physically but not a 'general' triangle. The general 'triangle' we reason about in geometry is *imagined*, and hence no measuring is involved.

Of course, as Piaget noted, young children are generally not yet capable of reasoning for themselves with the kind of 'formal operational' logic described above, but in primary school we can do much to prepare the way for children's mature geometrical thinking, and for their understanding of what 'doing geometry' involves. We can encourage children to *imagine* shapes and movements, we can encourage them to *generalize*, and we can encourage them to notice that there are significantly different ways of being 'correct' in mathematics, through ourselves always being careful how we answer the question, '***Why*** ...?' We can also teach children what doing geometry is *not*.

What geometrical reasoning is *not*

It is quite common for children to want to test a generalization such as 'the angles of any (flat) triangle add up to 180°', by drawing or choosing a particular triangle and measuring the angles with a protractor (or tearing off the corners of a particular paper triangle and re-arranging them in a line). There's possibly a feeling that lots of people could have done this in the past, and that every time anyone does it, they always come up with 180° – roughly. And so, if we could measure accurately enough, measuring lots of different kinds of particular triangles would eventually *prove* it.

This kind of activity is misleading for children in an important way. Working like this is how scientists work – by dealing with series of individual cases rather than reasoning about a *general* triangle, as mathematicians do. If all we did in geometry was measure actual particular triangles, however many triangles we measured practically – even assuming we could measure anything perfectly accurately (which we can't) – there would always be the possibility that in a triangle we haven't looked at yet, the angles might come to more or less than 180° – because we have no special *reason* for knowing it to be impossible.

In mathematics we reason *logically* about our generalizations using our imagination, and children will find that it is possible to reason logically that the angles of a flat triangle *must* add up to 180°, without doing any measuring at all[3]. And further, that if by measuring we come up with 181°, then the extra 1° is a measure of the *inaccuracy* inherent in our measuring; it is our measuring that is wrong.

As teachers, we don't help children understand what doing geometry is about if we encourage them to believe that the angles of a triangle really do add up to 180° because they've measured some triangles, or because they've torn the corners off one and arranged all three angles physically along a straight line. *Convincing them* is not the aim; *finding logical reasons* is.

Being logical is not to be confused with being conventional

Just as children need to learn the difference between measuring and being logical, they need to learn the difference between being conventionally 'correct' and being logically 'correct', as well. Being conventional is a matter of social agreement; being logical leads to a *necessary* acceptance of truth (it's not a matter of any kind of agreement).

The fact that three-sided polygons are called 'triangles' is a *social* agreement (they might have been called 'trilaterals'); that the exterior angles of any polygon add up to 360° (that is, one whole revolution) is *necessarily* true – there is no choice about it.

Have you tried drawing 'any polygon' yet, by the way? It is a two-dimensional closed shape, consisting of straight sides . . .[4]

We learn conventional names for things in geometry in the same way that we learn conventional names for things in any other walk of life, simply by agreeing to go along with what everyone else seems to call things. This makes our communicating 'correct' in a social sense, but not in a logical or necessary sense.

We can help children learn this important distinction through the ways that we answer their questions. This in turn will help children learn that there are different *kinds* of 'facts' in geometry, and therefore importantly different ways of being 'correct'.

3 The exterior angles of any triangle add up to 360° (because it is a polygon). Also, the combined interior and exterior angles at each vertex of a triangle add up to 180° (they make a straight line), so the total of all six exterior and interior angles together for any triangle will be 540° (i.e. 3 × 180°). Since we know that the exterior angles together account for 360° of this total, then the total for the interior angles together must be 180° (i.e. 540° – 360°).

4 Trying to draw a *general* polygon illustrates very well how mathematical objects are works of the imagination. We can define it, describe several of its visual properties, and develop valid theories about it, but *draw* it we cannot.

Because …

When children ask 'Why …?', teachers need to make sure they give the right kind of answer. If a child asks, 'Why are there 360° in a whole turn?' we need to say something like, 'Well, the Babylonians used to love numbers like 60 that you can divide up exactly without using fractions, so they thought 360 (6 x 60) was a really helpful number for dividing up a circle'. (Or something like that.) In other words, it's a convention and one can point to a social history …

If a child asks, 'Why do the angles of a quadrilateral add up to 360°?' we need to invite them to *reason* it through. 'Because by drawing a diagonal you can divide 'any quadrilateral' (a generalization again, in your head) into two triangles, and we know that the angles of a triangle always add up to 180°, so 2 × 180° = 360°.' It's *logical*; we have no choice.

If a child asks (pointing to a shape), 'Why is that a triangle?' we need to be careful to give a full answer. 'It's called a triangle because we've agreed to put *all* shapes like that one (all those flat, closed shapes with three straight sides) together into one group, and call them all 'tri-angles' – probably because they all have three angles as well.' It's an *agreement* that could have been otherwise.

And so as children work with and explore shapes and movements, and speculate and try things out, they will find themselves both 'correct' and 'wrong' in significantly different kinds of ways. The ways we that use the word 'because …' will help them develop important distinctions. Children need to know *in which way* they are 'right' or 'wrong', and that in the world of shapes, as with people, 'a rose by any other name would smell as sweet'.

Parts, properties, movements and definitions – the social basis of geometry

Definitions are social agreements in the same way as the names of the categories they define. We first *agree to define* categories in a particular way, and then later use those categories in our classifying and reasoning. Doing mathematics is the shared occupation of a social community, and within mathematics definitions are *chosen* (and hence allowed to change).

We tend to use parts and properties that we distinguish within shapes and movements to define our conventional categories, and so early work with children involves inviting them first to agree to our *distinctions between* certain parts, properties and movements before doing any categorizing based on these. None of this yet involves logical necessity; it is still only about inviting social agreement.

Initially children seem to distinguish between shapes that are named for them in a *holistic* way, simply learning, '*That's* (called) a triangle' and '*That's* (called) a square' and so on, without distinguishing any parts[5]. Gradually their discrimination becomes finer and they are able to distinguish **parts** such as 'corners' and 'lines' that they can later agree to call 'vertices' and 'sides' and so on. Later still children will begin to notice how parts relate to each other to give shapes **properties**, e.g. a trapezium has just two sides that are parallel to each other, or adjacent sides of a rectangle meet at 90°. Children also learn to distinguish **movements** from one another, e.g. between turning a shape around (rotating), and turning it over (reflecting).

5 See Van Hiele, P. M. (1985) *Structure and Insight. A Theory of Mathematics Education.* Orlando: Orlando Academic Press

So as young children make and handle shapes, fit them together, and move them (and themselves) around, they gradually learn to *join in* with the conventional language we offer them to describe the distinctions they see and notice with us. We invite their agreement to joining in with the language that reflects the distinctions and definitions the rest of us currently use; all of this is social activity – and the agreements could always be otherwise[6].

Using transformations and invariants to name and define

By playing with, handling, and fitting together collections of physical shapes children will be using the Euclidean transformations of rotation, reflection, and translation. This is a world in which lengths, angles, and areas all stay the same (invariant, constant), and are therefore features *constantly available to be noticed* as shapes are moved around and fitted together.

By including similar physical shapes as well as congruent ones in the collection, the transformation of **scaling** can be imagined. (Note the transformation of scaling affects a previous invariant: area.)

Under the transformations of rotation, reflection, translation, and scaling together, the angles of a square stay the same – they are invariant – as are the **ratios** of lengths to each other. Paying attention to just these invariants leads to a 'square' being defined in our geometry as a polygon with *four right-angles* and *four equal sides*. These invariants can be used to define the shape. As the actual lengths of the equal sides and the area all change under scaling, we don't use the changing attributes of individual lengths or area, which vary, in defining a square.

Triangles are a different challenge to organize – there are many kinds of triangle, whereas there is only one kind of square. Children need to make and meet many different kinds of triangle before they can realize[7] again that what stays invariant in any kind of triangle under rotation, reflection, translation, and scaling are the angles and the ratios of sides. They will notice that no one seems to care how long individual sides are, or how big the angles: as long as there are three of those things making this closed, flat shape everyone calls a 'triangle'.

Significantly, noticing what stays the same and what changes as we transform something leads naturally to generalizing. In effect, children are learning to use terms such as 'triangle', 'square', 'oblong', 'circle' and so on in ways that acknowledge that, for example, 'a triangle' (that is, *any* triangle) is a closed shape with three straight sides forming three angles. These are the *invariants* of 'a triangle' in the geometry we begin with at school; any other properties

6 To help children realize this, one very nice activity is to invite them to make as many different pentagonal shapes as they can, and then to sort these into different kinds of pentagon themselves - also inventing names for the categories they make. Since there is no conventional tradition for this (as there are for triangles and for quadrilaterals), the experience can illustrate very well to children the fact that names, categories and definitions of shapes are all simply social agreements – which could always be otherwise. (Thank you David Fielker, (1981) *Removing the Shackles of Euclid* Derby: ATM.)

7 They are unlikely to be realizing this consciously, or be capable of expressing what they see in these terms. What they are *noticing* – informally – is that the 'corners' don't change however you move the shape about, and that it still *looks* as if it's the same shape (i.e. it's what we call 'similar') whenever we do those things with it.

that you might notice when you look at a particular triangle (e.g. this one's got a right angle) could *change*, yet the shape would still be a triangle. Similarly, it doesn't matter 'which way up' a triangle is (that is, how it is rotated), it will still be a triangle. Orientation can *change*; 'having a point at the top' is not an invariant property of triangles in the geometry we use.

It is clear how physical experiences with a wide range of *dynamic* materials are essential for children doing geometry. The active making, moving, describing, transforming and combining of physical shapes that children do with physical and IT materials forms the vital basis of their flexible *imagining* and forming of categories.

Gradually, through meeting, making and moving shapes in their activities and discussing what they and we see changing and staying the same, children learn to use words (category names) in the same ways that we do. These distinctions and agreed categories then become formalized into definitions.

Definitions essentially spell out explicitly the agreed boundaries around a category; they are a kind of *verbal contract* underlying discussion that is always open to revision and scrutiny. 'Triangles' become defined as, 'closed, flat shapes having exactly three straight sides' for as long as it suits us to look at them that way[8].

In our **Glossary** we list the definitions that are usually agreed for work in primary schools. Notice how important your visual imagination is to you as you read these agreements, and remind yourself just how important children's physical experiences with actions and movements are to them, as you discuss and invite them to agree with the conventions you suggest.

8 If we move to another kind of geometry, perhaps with shapes on curved surfaces, we might want to change our definition of 'triangle'.

From defining towards classifying and relating

It is one thing to be able to distinguish and name shapes (and parts and properties of shapes), but it is quite another to be able to relate such categories to each other and to reason with such relations. Being clear about categories is fundamental to thinking logically with them.

In schools in some countries much early discussion with children focuses explicitly on 'different *kinds* of things' (or categories), relations between categories, and hierarchies of categories, so that children's attention is consciously drawn to the importance of category distinctions for logical thinking. This becomes important with children doing geometry as we introduce them to relationships between categories of shapes and the ways in which inclusive hierarchies of categories lead to the possibilities of reasoning with ever broader generalizations[9]. Putting things into categories and relating those categories to each other is called *classifying*, and classifying shapes is one key way in which we put a conventional order and structure onto the many possible worlds of geometries.

Sometimes category distinctions are very subtle. *Logically* we can't add different *kinds* of things together; '3 m 15 cm' is not 18 anythings, it's *either* 315 cm or 3.15 m. Children will encounter this logical feature again when they try adding

9 E.g. polygon → quadrilateral → rectangle → square, is one such inclusive hierarchy of categories, enabling us to *deduce* logically that the sum of the exterior angles of a square will add up to 360°, for example, because those of *all* polygons do, and a square is one kind of polygon.

together, for example, $\frac{1}{4}$ and $\frac{2}{3}$. Conventionally however, we often say '3 metres 15 centimetres' as if we've 'added' them together, whereas we've simply put them *next to* each other, one after the other, not combined them.

And so to generalizing in geometry …

In doing geometry, having agreed categories and definitions we then reason about mathematical objects and their relationships *in general*, such as 'a polygon', 'a quadrilateral' or 'a cylinder' or 'a sphere', and these generalized objects are similar kinds of things to those other mathematical objects we ask children to make – pure numbers, such as '6', or '23', or '⁻0·5'. As in number and algebra, in doing geometry we *reason* with our *generalizations* (whereas in measuring we're always measuring something specific, something particular).

What children importantly become better at as they work and develop through their primary years is the *virtual* action essential to generalizing – they gradually become able to reason about '*any* quadrilateral' and so on, and it is only possible to do this in our *imaginations*. Any quadrilateral that we actually make or draw is always a particular one; the important *general* quadrilateral that we want children to be able to reason about can only be constructed in our heads, and the same goes for all the other geometrical generalizations we want children to make. In this important sense, geometry can only be done in our heads.

Notice that it's more difficult to imagine a general triangle, or quadrilateral, or polygon, or prism, than it is to imagine a general square; that's because there are many different *kinds* of triangle, quadrilateral, and so on, but only one kind of square (in our conventional classification). Again in this, the variety and range of children's physical actions, and the maximum use of *dynamic* materials (such as geo strips) is essential; the more *transforming* children can do physically as they notice and discuss what changes and what stays the same, the better.

When doing practical geometry with children always encourage them towards generalizing with questions like, 'Will that *always* work …?', and 'What if …?'. And encourage their reasoning with questions like, 'Is that because …?', and 'Why is that, I wonder …?' And don't feel that some children are too young to be able to contemplate such questions; even before children are capable of answering them, the *habit of asking* such questions in one's teaching is what is important[10]. It is for the children to do the generalizing, the reasoning and the imagining.

Working in 2D and 3D

Essentially, working with shapes and space in three dimensions rather than two involves no change in approach. Work in 3D begins with children handling, rotating, reflecting, and translating shapes in various ways, and also noting that scaling only changes lengths, surface areas and volumes. A cube is a cube is a cube, however big or small it is. Angles are invariant under these four kinds of transformation, as are ratios of lengths. Fitting 3D shapes together is also a key explorative activity.

10 'The palace of reason has to be entered by the courtyard of habit.' See Peters, R. S. (1966) *Ethics and Education*. London: George, Allen & Unwin p314. For Peters, this was what he called 'the paradox of education'.

Some agreements on names are changed in a shift from 2D to 3D work, and some interpretations of transformations shift up a dimension. So for example, 'sides' become 'edges' in 3D, a 'rotation' would be around a line (instead of a point) and a 'reflection' would be around a plane (instead of around a line). Curved surfaces become notable in 3D, as opposed to curved lines in 2D. These are all conventional agreements we invite children to join in with, as their experiences in 3D invite new *discriminations between* parts and properties, prior to agreeing to use these discriminations in new definitions (see **Glossary**).

Once 3D categories are agreed (e.g. 'polyhedra', 'prisms'), children can begin to relate categories to each other, to classify, to *generalize* and to reason *logically* about aspects of three-dimensional space. Reasoning about the possibilities of tiling in two dimensions, for example, shifts up to reasoning about the possibilities of packing in three dimensions.

Activities directly connecting 2D and 3D parts, properties, transformations and shapes are invaluable. So in the early years, printing with 3D shapes offers important connections between 2D shapes and 3D 'faces', and later on work on the 'nets' of 3D shapes does the same.

Essentially, work in 3D involves the same developmental sequence of activities as work in 2D: *discriminating between* parts, properties, and transformations in order to agree conventional *definitions*; *generalizing* from such definitions; *imagining* 'a (general) cylinder', 'a prism' and so on, and thence to *reasoning logically* about such mathematical objects.

Walking the line ... a difference of perspective

Finally, much geometry activity is done from the point of view of 'looking *at*' shapes, and moving them around in front of us and so on. It is quite often very helpful however to shift perspective and to imagine walking around, along, and inside shapes. Young children do this readily and actually in climbing frames and playground equipment, but often, in school, activities are done on tables with materials in their hands, which almost exclusively involves 'looking *at*'.

Programmable robots and the programming language 'Logo', however, allow us to explore shape properties, and position and direction in ways that invoke the 'walking along and inside shapes' perspective to good effect. And a shift in perspective often makes different things clear, and familiar things look helpfully different.

When children are 'looking *at*' polygons, for example, the only angles that are obvious are the interior angles. When they try making a polygon with a Logo turtle however, all of a sudden it's the unwritten exterior angles that become important – and the 'total turtle trip' experience travelling around such a shape allows children to appreciate how *all* the exterior angles *must* add up to 360°, in a very different and immediate way.

Encourage children to shift perspectives frequently, and thus to unite experience of 'position' and 'direction' closely with what are often thought of as the more 'static' aspects of shape.

Doing geometry – using Cartesian coordinates

René Descartes (1596–1650) is generally credited with inventing a system for describing a position in space using axes and a set of numbers, called coordinates. This revolutionary idea subsequently allowed algebra and geometry to become united so that equations could be interpreted visually, and shapes could be defined and explored with algebraic equations.

Doing geometry with coordinates - uniting geometry with algebra – is usually called 'analytic geometry', with René Descartes credited as its father. Analytic geometry is developed systematically in secondary school mathematics, but children begin to meet this approach with us as they are introduced to Cartesian coordinates in Geometry, Measurement and Statistics 4.

Geometry in Geometry, Measurement and Statistics 1

Both artists and mathematicians pay attention to shapes, and lines, and forms in the physical world. When teaching geometry though, it helps to remember that artists and mathematicians pay attention in different ways. Mathematicians' primary concern in geometry is to render a physical world predictable, and so the shapes and lines and forms selected for early mathematical attention are those that are potentially *predictable*.

Straight lines are predictable, as are regular curves; we know where we are going if we 'walk along' them. Although when teaching art we might discuss the varied forms and outlines of clouds with children, mathematicians save the complexity of weather forecasting for post-graduate study (and still have much to do on that). Geometry in school is restricted to the study of **parts** and **properties** of only those shapes that are formed with straight lines and/or regular curves.

So in Geometry, Measurement and Statistics 1 children are invited to be active in various ways with simple, predictable and common 2D and 3D shapes. Three aspects are important at any primary level though: the **transformations** involved, the **invariants**, and the associated **communicating** that is developed in discussion.

The transformations

The four kinds of transformation children use in activities at this level are: rotations, translations, reflections and scaling. At this stage these are discussed intuitively and informally with children as they make and handle a variety of regular and irregular shapes.

Rotation: children are invited to turn shapes 'around', 'upside down' and so on – and to turn themselves around – to experience what changes, and what stays the same, as *orientation* alters.

Translation: children are invited to move both shapes and themselves to, from, and between various positions, and in various directions.

Reflection: although children are not invited to think about and explore line symmetry explicitly, they may well 'turn shapes over' in the course of making patterns and so on and thus 'reflect' them in practice.

Scaling: children work with shapes in various sizes (that is, shapes that are similar to each other) and thus have opportunities to notice what changes, and what stays the same, as only 'size' changes.

The invariants

The parts and properties of shapes that we invite children to notice particularly at this level are *invariants* under the above four transformations.

At this stage children are not expected to be able to say things like 'the angles stay the same' under all these transformations, but they would be expected to be able to *sort shapes successfully* into categories such as 'triangles', 'squares', 'oblongs', 'cubes', 'pyramids' and so on, regardless of their size and orientation. They are very unlikely to be able to explain *why* a pyramid is still a pyramid if it is upside down (or twice as big as this other one), but they can in a practical, intuitive way show *in their sorting* that they are able to discriminate between different 'shapes' on the basis of those parts and properties that 'stay the same' as we scale up or down, rotate, translate, or reflect in a broad, holistic way.

Distances, angles (and consequently areas and volumes) are invariant under rotations, reflections and translations. Under scaling, angles and ratios of lines (and consequently things like parallel lines) stay the same.

The communicating

Discussion needs to be relatively open and informal as children work at this early level, introducing conventional terms as and when children seek to *discriminate* between, describe, explain and name what they see and do. Children shouldn't have 'correct' (that is, conventional) names and terms imposed on them at this stage; invite children to agree to use conventional vocabulary as it becomes useful to them in describing what they see.

In particular, agreeing conventional *categories* of shapes is important, and you will need to remember that, e.g. the category of 'triangles' is much more complicated to distinguish for children than that of 'squares' (there are many different kinds of triangle, yet only one kind of square).

The conventional category 'rectangles' is also especially problematic, since technically it includes the category of 'squares'. Young children often have difficulties with 'inclusion' relations between categories. It is perfectly acceptable for children to distinguish the category of 'oblongs'. **The combining of 'oblongs' with 'squares' to agree the inclusive category 'rectangles'** needs to be discussed fully with children, since for some the idea that a shape can have two different names is confusing ('How can that be both a square *and* a rectangle?'). Also, it is very common in everyday discussion for people to speak as if the term 'rectangle' meant only 'oblong'. Allow children plenty of time to absorb a technically-correct *inclusive* definition of 'rectangle'.

Please see individual activity groups (and **Glossary**) for lists of the particular conventional terms likely to be introduced during particular Geometry, Measurement and Statistics 1 activities.

Key mathematical ideas: Measurement and statistics in the primary years

Underlying the activities in Geometry, Measurement and Statistics 1 are many key mathematical ideas that children will be developing and extending, as well as some conventions they may be meeting for the first time.

In order to teach these ideas effectively, those who are working on the activities with children will need to be clear themselves about the mathematical ideas and about which activities address which ideas.

The following section includes a brief outline of the key mathematical ideas that children will be encountering in the Measurement and statistics activity groups of the *Geometry, Measurement and Statistics 1 Teaching Resource Handbook*. The introductory page for each activity group lists the key mathematical ideas associated with each activity. As you prepare for your teaching, you may find it helpful to remind yourself about the key ideas behind each activity by referring to this section.

The mathematics coordinator may also find it useful to work on the key mathematical ideas in professional development sessions with the class teachers and the wider school staff.

Introduction

It is important to remember that doing geometry, measurement, and using statistics are significantly related aspects of mathematics, and that each of these areas of activity has strong connections with the other two. It is important to remember too that all three also have strong connections with number, pattern, and calculating activity.

'Geometry' in ancient Greek means 'earth measurement'; many physical measures involve geometrical ideas (e.g. pressure is usually measured per 'square' unit), and patterns in data (themselves usually records of measuring activity) are commonly represented visually – as are numbers themselves, of course, in the form of a number line.

Each of these areas of mathematical activity also has its own distinctive concerns: shapes are commonly classified with little reference to their size; we measure time, force, and temperature as well as distance, area, and volume, and in statistics we are often concerned to interpret and illustrate a 'significance' in identified relationships. In what follows we treat these three broad areas of mathematical activity relatively separately for ease of reference to their key ideas, but when you are teaching each area be sure to exploit inter-connections at every opportunity.

Measurement and statistics in the primary years

We always measure for a *purpose*, that is, measuring something is never an end in itself. Because of this, children's experiences with measuring are most effective when set within purposeful contexts, for example when reviewing an arrangement of classroom furniture we could ask, 'I wonder if that bookcase would fit in that gap over there?' Similarly, measuring mass/weight and volume or capacity has a clear purpose when cooking, or in any other situation where we might want to be able to repeat something. Timing is important for organizing deadlines and appointments. Cross-curricular links generally are invaluable for offering great varieties of purpose to children's measuring activity.

There is another consequence of measuring being purposeful that can be overlooked in primary school activities: our measuring in life is always only as formal, or informal, as accurate, or approximate, as suits the particular measuring *purpose*, on any occasion. As adults, we do not usually measure our drink of coffee at home in millilitres, nor do teenagers measure how far apart to put their coats down in metres when making a 'goal' for a game in the park. Standard units do not become appropriate to measuring tasks simply because children are of a certain age, or because they appear from some point onwards in a curriculum; standard units are not somehow 'grown-up' or 'proper' measuring and should not be introduced as such.

Standard units are used only on particular occasions *for particular reasons*, usually to ensure clear communication, and/or when there is a lack of personal trust. When trying out a new recipe we usually measure the named amounts precisely, because we don't yet trust our own judgement in the new venture; standard measures are very important agreements in global trade, and in scientific communication – both contexts in which 'trust' depends crucially upon careful use of agreed units. We might not use standard measures for our drinks at home, but we certainly expect them in shops.

If children are to fully understand measuring, the aspect of *purpose* – and its consequences - needs to feature clearly in all work and discussions. Standard units are not the 'best' units, nor are they the 'most accurate'; they are simply the units most appropriate to particular occasions. Probably we do more measuring in everyday life without standard units; children need to recognize why they use the types of units they do when they are measuring in all types of situations. Standard units are necessary only for *communicating* and for supporting *trust*; children need to learn *when* standard units are appropriate, in context.

Measuring – contrasting and comparing

There is a sense in which all measuring can be understood as comparing, in that an underlying purpose in our measuring action is always to compare **qualities** or **quantities**. Interestingly, not all comparing involves measuring – sometimes we count, and sometimes we order, to compare (the number of votes in an election, or the winners of a race for example).

It is worth noting that we can't do any comparing until we have first distinguished whatever quality is to be compared. Thus contrasting qualities (distinguishing between them) is an essential prerequisite to comparing, and so sorting, and distinguishing between, in topics such as length and capacity, different kinds of 'big' and 'small', are crucial preparatory activities with young children.

Measuring and counting – continuous and discrete quantities

There is an important difference between the two questions, 'How much?' and 'How many?' To answer the first, we measure; to answer the second, we count. **We measure continuous amounts, but we count discrete objects.** We measure time, length, area, volume and so on, but we count votes, cars, and the number of items in our basket.

This distinction is important – it leads to the consequence that where measuring involves a continuous quantity, the outcome is always an *approximate* figure. And this observation itself has important implications for our use of continuous measuring scales and instruments, and for always having to decide on an appropriate level of accuracy in any situation. It also has very important connections with the work we do with children on fractions and interpreting the spaces between whole numbers on a number line.

There are a variety of questions that ask about 'how much' of something we have, and thus lead us to measure: 'how far' and 'how long' ask about length, or distance, or time; 'how heavy' asks about weight/mass. 'Where is ...?' is a question that can invite a combination of measures, e.g. an angle and a distance. Volume, capacity and mass all tend to be asked about with the broad question itself, 'How much?' (e.g. 'How much sugar would you like in that?').

Children thus need to learn to use a wide variety of terms and language in association with purposeful measuring and comparing, including the usual grammatical distinction between having 'less' of something continuous, or having 'fewer' discrete things.

Measuring and types of scales

There are important distinctions between different types of measuring scales that have implications for the kinds of calculating we can do with measurements we have made, and thus for the types of statistics we can do with measures and counts of various kinds.

As a handy reference, in 1946[11] S. S. Stevens proposed a classification of measures that has proved very productive in stimulating debate, and that also connects usefully with our approaches to data handling and measuring. It is worth considering not only because of the connection with statistics, but because it explains why although 20 cm is 'twice as long' as 10 cm, 20 °C is not 'twice as hot' as 10 °C (that is, we can't do the same calculations with temperature readings on the Celsius scale that we can do with lengths). Stevens' classification is not put forward here as a 'correct' view of measuring, but simply as one that has an interesting and helpful relevance to the development of both measuring and statistics work with children.

As a psychologist, Stevens was much concerned with statistics, and his classification is thus concerned with both measuring and handling data in the contexts of physical and social science. In statistics, both measuring and counting are used in contrasting (that is, distinguishing between) and comparing.

The Stevens (1946) classification distinguishes four types of 'measuring' scale:

- **Nominal**: this involves simply distinguishing between (contrasting) and putting items into different categories, according to names or specific qualities, e.g. distinguishing between male/female, or distinguishing between English/French/Spanish, and so on, as different modern European languages. Distinguishing between team players by giving them different numbers on their shirts is a kind of nominal scale. Importantly, no ordering or value is involved or implied.
- **Ordinal**: an ordinal scale distinguishes between and also *ranks* items qualitatively, but without attending to any degree of difference between ranks, that is, such a scale simply compares qualities of objects or events by position in an order. The Beaufort scale of wind strength is one example, as is the Mohs scale of mineral hardness. Social surveys often use ordinal scales when asking people if they 'agree strongly', 'agree', 'don't mind', 'disagree', 'disagree strongly', and so on.
- **Interval**: an interval scale discriminates between values, and orders them, but also focuses on constant *degrees* of difference between values on the scale. Examples are temperatures in °C, or dates on an infinite timeline. The intervals on the scale – e.g. in degrees or years – are all the same as each other, so *differences between* temperatures or dates can be computed and added or subtracted (and ratios *of differences* make sense), but we can't sensibly 'add' or 'multiply' with dates or temperatures themselves. On 1 January 2010 we could say that 1 January 2000 was 'twice *as long ago*' as 1 January 2005 (that is, a ratio of differences between dates), but we cannot compare two dates (or temperatures) directly themselves

11 Stevens, S. S. (1946) *On the Theory of Scales of Measurement*, in Science, **103** (2684): 677–680

with each other in any other way apart from simply ordering them and saying how far apart they are[12].

- **Ratio**: a ratio scale distinguishes 'difference', 'order', and 'degrees of difference', but also includes an important, non-negotiable 'zero' boundary that actually leads to different possibilities of calculating[13]. The classic examples of ratio scales include our physical measures of length, area, volume and mass wherein it makes no sense to think of 'negative' lengths, areas, and so on[14]. Importantly, this also means that differences between values on a ratio scale are also values themselves, and we can thus make sense of *ratios* of particular *values* to each other, e.g. a difference between two lengths is itself a length (whereas a difference between two dates on an interval scale, is not itself a 'date'). We can compare two different values on a ratio scale in *two* ways: we can say that 6 cm is 4 cm longer than 2 cm (their difference), but we can also say that 6 cm is three times as long as 2 cm (their ratio).

The above classification might seem a rather complicated background to work in primary schools, but it can actually help draw attention to several key basic ideas in measuring and comparing, and is highly relevant to the kinds of questions and data handling with which many primary children can engage.

Notice that Stevens' classification is cumulative; first we pay attention only to *differences* between items, and we simply *distinguish between* various qualities. We can thus make categories. This 'nominal' scale relates closely to children's early sorting activities, to their early distinguishing of qualities such as 'heaviness', and 'volume' as refinements from their early global use of terms such as 'big' and 'small'.

Secondly, by using an 'ordinal' scale we still distinguish between items and qualities but we now *order* these categories or qualities as well. This relates to children's early comparing and ordering of lengths, heaviness, volumes, and so on.

Thirdly, the idea of repeated equal *units* and specified *values* on an 'interval' scale is introduced, and the combining of (adding) and finding differences between (subtracting) values becomes possible. This relates to children meeting the idea of measuring 'units', adding and comparing lengths and so on, and introduces the possibility of meaningful 'negative' values.

And finally, once scales that have all the previous properties *and* a fixed 'zero' boundary are introduced, *ratios* of values become meaningful comparisons. This relates to children progressing from 'additive' thinking to the crucial further possibilities of 'multiplicative' thinking in relation to measures.

Thus there is a close correlation between Stevens' proposed classification and the development of measuring and statistics with children. First we invite children simply to ***discriminate*** *between* various qualities (general sorting;

12 This is actually because in practice there is no necessary, fixed 'zero' point on an interval scale, and both positive and negative values can potentially be thought of as 'going on forever' either side of an arbitrary 'zero'. In later physics, children will meet the Kelvin temperature scale with its 'absolute zero' and also the idea of a 'Big Bang' and 'zero time'.

13 Interestingly, it is the importance of 'starting from zero', e.g. when we measure length with a ruler, that children often do not appreciate immediately.

14 We will also leave discussion of negative values within quantum physics and the notion of 'anti-matter' for another occasion; we're just doing primary mathematics at the moment!

noting qualities such as heaviness, extension, heat and so on). Then we introduce the idea of ***ordering*** various degrees or levels of those qualities (***comparing***: e.g. longer than, shorter than and so on). Next we introduce *equal* ordered degrees of difference in qualities (that is, intervals or ***units***), and thus the possibility of adding and subtracting (comparing) differences, and *naming* individual amounts (***values*** on a scale). Finally, with ratio scales we introduce the full possibilities of comparing (adding and subtracting) values themselves and ***ratios*** of values with multiplicative thinking.

Together these activities and objects (in bold, above) constitute the key aspects of measuring in the primary years, and can be used as key focuses for attention both in teaching and in judging children's progress. These are, as it were, the *roots* of measuring activity. Notice how in teaching, these key focuses are approached in the same order as Stevens' cumulative classification of scales.

A special note about money

Stevens' classification has been valuable for the amount of productive debate it has engendered, but a weakness in it is possibly revealed when we ask which type of scale applies to money. In terms of *cash*, money is measured with a ratio scale; you can't have 'negative cash'. But of course you can *owe* money, and that makes money seem more like an interval scale; 'zero' money becomes a fairly arbitrary point when you're a student, and both debt and riches appear to stretch potentially endlessly in either direction. Some *ratio* comparisons still work: £10 is still 'twice as much as' £5, and owing £10 means owing 'twice as much as' owing £5, but 'how many times' as much money have you got if you *have* £10 as opposed to when you *owe* £10?

It is worth noting as well that money is not 'continuous' in the same sense that time, length, area, volume, mass and so on are considered to be. Thus *actual* amounts of money (like cash) are exact (not approximate), even though we see around us currency exchange rates quoted such as £1 = $1·51715.

Money is included as a 'measure' (of economic worth) in the curriculum, but the ways in which it is used and calculated are significantly different to other physical measures.

The physical measures

The physical measures introduced during primary schooling in England are: length, mass and weight, volume and capacity, time, temperature, area, and speed.

Length and distance: Technically, when we measure 'length' we measure what would perhaps be better called 'linear extension', and confusingly for children, in everyday life linear extension gets called different things in different contexts. Height, width, depth, length, and distance are all different ways of referring to the same quality of linear extension, and so children need to connect references to their 'height' and how 'tall' they are, with the 'depth' of a swimming pool, the 'width' of their bedroom, the 'length' of a football pitch, and with how 'far' it is to the shops, as all measures of 'the same thing'. Much discussion is needed around this great variety of language use, and also around the wide variety of instruments used to measure different 'lengths' and 'distances' in different contexts.

Gradually, children will learn that there is also an important distinction between 'distance' and 'displacement' when measuring 'how far' it is from A to B. 'Distance' is simply an

amount (a magnitude, e.g. how far you actually have to travel), whereas 'displacement' is both a magnitude *and* a direction (called a vector generally, and a 'translation' in geometry). In everyday life we describe the displacement between two places as the linear distance between them 'as the crow flies'; we assume crows fly along the shortest (straight) path between two points, whereas, e.g. the distance from our home to school will be further than 'the crow flies' because we won't be able to travel in a straight line. Because displacement is a straight-line path, we are able to specify it as movement in a constant direction. This distinction is obviously crucial in answering, 'How far is it from A to B?'.

There are interesting later developments in measuring 'distance' on a global scale; the shortest distance between, say, London and Los Angeles lies along what's called a 'great circle'[15] (a section, or arc of a circle drawn around the earth with its centre at the centre of the earth). Aircraft generally navigate along great circles, but typically if we are asked to say how far away Los Angeles is from London we are more likely to say it's '11 hours' away, than 5,452 miles. This also connects with the measuring of astronomical distances in 'light years'; when distances are large, the 'distance' from A to B becomes more meaningfully expressed in lengths of time than in units of 'linear extension'.

The standard SI unit of linear extension in all contexts is the metre (m). Length is measured with ratio scales (metric or imperial), since 'zero length' is an absolute. Consequently, ratios of lengths to each other make good sense, and are used frequently in both everyday life and in science.

15 Or it would be if the earth were actually a sphere; for all practical purposes we treat it as if it is.

Mass and weight: The 'mass' of a physical object is the pleasingly simple idea of 'how much of it' (that is, the material stuff) you've got; measuring this directly however, is not so simple. In practice, as Isaac Newton (1643–1727) pointed out, we take advantage of the fact that under the effect of gravity *weight* and *mass* are directly proportional to each other, that is, if you double the 'amount of stuff' you've got you will find that it now weighs twice as much as it did.

What this means is that (unless we are out in space) we can compare the masses of two objects with each other by comparing their weights; if a proud new father weighs 22 times as much as his newly born daughter, then we can be sure that his 'mass' is 22 times greater than hers (there is 22 times 'as much' of him as there is of her).

The standard SI unit of mass is the kilogram (kg) and in order to measure mass we do in practice compare objects with this standard unit by 'weighing' them – that is, by comparing their weights with the *weight* of a 1 kg mass. 'Weight' however is a force; it is the gravitational force acting upon any object, and in imperial units it is measured in 'pounds' (lb) and 'ounces' (oz). In the metric system the force due to gravity, that is, 'weight', is measured in 'newtons' (N).

The designers of space stations have to do their calculations based on the knowledge that in orbit the masses of everyone involved will not have changed, even though their weights will have. The force of a collision between two astronauts in space does not change however (it hurts just as much), because their masses do not change; even though each is weightless, two astronauts' bodies still have as much momentum when moving in space as they did on earth (and therefore will take just as much stopping).

In school, using the correct language for the metric system can sound odd because it is not the everyday language children meet outside school. In the everyday world we do compare masses by 'weighing' them, but technically we should not go on to say that the 'weight' of something is so many kilograms – that's its *mass*.

So teachers have something of a problem in deciding whether to use the scientific language of physics as they talk about the SI units of mass (kg), or whether to carry on talking about the 'weights' of objects in kilograms and – in everyday language - pretend that kilograms are units of weight. Many teachers talk of 'heaviness' to avoid using the word 'weight', and do indeed ask children to 'compare masses'. In Geometry, Measurement and Statistics 1 we recommend that you follow common everyday language use. In the subsequent Geometry, Measurement and Statistics teaching resource Handbooks, the term 'mass' is used throughout in relation to its related units of measure: grams and kilograms.

Both mass and weight are measured with ratio scales, since their 'zeros' are absolute. Ratios of masses and weights to each other make good sense, and are used frequently in both everyday life and in science.

Volume and capacity: 'Volume' is the amount of space something occupies, whereas 'capacity' is how much space there is inside a vessel or container of some sort, or how much volume it could 'hold'. In the metric system, the volumes of liquids are usually measured in litres (e.g. drinks, petrol), and the volumes of solid objects in cubic metres (m^3); capacities are typically measured in m^3, but can also be expressed in litres (e.g. a 1 ℓ bottle). 1 litre (ℓ) is equivalent to 0·001 m^3 (one thousandth of a cubic metre). Measuring either volume or capacity in m^3 introduces children to what is called a 'derived' measure; the unit of volume (or capacity) is *derived* from the so-called 'base measure' for length (m)[16].

Interestingly, 1 ℓ of pure water has a mass of 1 kg. Both 'volume' and 'mass' are in a sense measures of 'how much' of something you've got, but 'mass' is the basic scientific SI unit for how much 'matter' there is, whereas 'volume' judges 'how much you've got' by measuring the amount of space something takes up. In everyday life we tend to use 'weights' and 'volumes' for all practical purposes, e.g. buying and selling, cooking and so on.

In science, where 'how much matter' (or material substance) you are dealing with is generally much more important than the space it is occupying, we use kilograms to measure how much 'material' there is of an object. When we want a drink, we are generally much more interested in how much volume we will be given.

The capacities of containers and vessels are usually measured by calculating using the three dimensions of space (e.g. length, width, and depth), or by filling them with a known volume of liquid. Capacities are then typically quoted in both m^3 and in litres.

The volumes of liquids are usually measured inside graduated containers (or through pumps), or in the case of solid objects of awkward dimensions, volumes of objects can be measured by using a displacement vessel.

16 For this reason it is usually more effective to introduce children to litres before 'cubic' measures for volume and capacity; calculating with *derived* measures (e.g. m^3) depends upon a good facility with multiplying if the effort of the arithmetic involved is not to prove a distraction for children.

Both volume and capacity are measured with ratio scales, since their 'zeros' are absolute. Consequently, ratios of volumes (and capacities) to each other make good sense, and are used frequently in both everyday life and in science – particularly in the repetition of mixtures in specified proportions.

Time: There are several aspects to the topic of 'time': telling the time, duration, succession, and speed. As a compound measure, 'speed' is addressed formally in the final year of primary schooling, although it will certainly come up in children's everyday conversations from an early age as they are asked to 'go faster' or more 'slowly' or 'quickly', and as they experience 'racing' in a variety of forms.

There are two central ideas that children need to connect together for effective development of their understanding of how we measure time: the idea of *linear* time, and the idea of a repeating *cycle*. Linear time is the sense that 'time' stretches both backwards into history and pre-history forever, and endlessly forwards into an infinite future. The key visual illustration of this is the 'timeline' – which bears an uncanny resemblance to the number line, even down to the fact that there is an identified 'zero' point for most cultures, 'before' and 'after' which 'things were different'. In the activity goups we refer to these times as BCE and CE: before common era and common era.

Work with timelines connects well with children's developing understanding of numbers as distances along a number line, and with their appreciation of different kinds of numbers; the ideas of 'order' and 'succession' are crucial in this.

Since any timeline includes an 'arbitrary' zero point (it could have been chosen differently), the line becomes an *interval* scale stretching potentially infinitely either side of zero. As such, ratios of dates to each other don't make sense, only ratios of *lengths* of time (durations) to each other; 4 hours is twice as long as 2 hours, but 4 July is not 'twice as' anything in relation to 2 July.

The idea of repeating 'cycles' is closely related to our experiences in a constantly-changing natural world of moon cycles, daily (sun) cycles, and seasons. We use such natural cycles in our everyday measuring of time as we plan 'summer' holidays, prepare for important dates with our calendar, sleep 'at night' and so on. The hands of an analogue clock illustrate to children constantly how we measure time in repeating cycles.

Since both linear time and repeating cycles are crucial to how we deal with succession, duration, and telling the time, children need *both* kinds of illustration prominently as we work with them on measuring time.

Since time is also sensed rather more indirectly (unlike heaviness, volume, and sheer physical size), because the scale of time ranges so widely from instants to eons, and because our awareness of how fast 'time is passing' changes so much depending on context and mood, children are also particularly dependent on discussion, illustrations and active experiences with instruments to develop their personal understanding of time.

The standard SI unit of time is the 'second' (s).

Temperature: Temperature is a measure of how 'hot' or 'cold' something (or someone) is[17], and is measured in degrees on the Celsius (°C), Fahrenheit (°F), or Kelvin (K) scales. In Europe and in much of the world the Celsius scale is generally used in everyday life; in the USA the Fahrenheit scale is commonly preferred. In much of science, the SI unit of K (Kelvin) is used. Degrees Kelvin are equivalent in size to degrees Celsius, but the zero of the Kelvin scale is a theoretical 'absolute' zero meaning there are no 'minus' temperature values possible in K.

The Celsius scale is based around the freezing point (0°C) of pure water (at one atmosphere of pressure, or sea level) and the corresponding boiling point (100°C). Thus children will probably first experience the idea of 'negative' values (or 'minus' numbers) in the context of 'below zero' winter temperatures in either °C or (much more rarely) °F, and/or ice in everyday life, and this is a very helpful context to use when introducing negative numbers.

Since the Celsius scale includes an 'arbitrary' zero point (that is, it could have been chosen differently), it is an *interval* scale stretching potentially[18] infinitely either side of zero. As such, ratios of individual temperature values in °C or °F to each other don't make sense, only ratios of temperature *differences* on these scales; a drop of 6°C is twice as big a drop as one of 3°C, but $^{-}6$°C is not 'twice as cold' as $^{-}3$°C.

Children are very well aware of temperature through their senses from an early age, and so work in primary school is mainly directed to introducing the Celsius scale, and experiencing various types of thermometer. Many children will be familiar with mercury or alcohol-in-glass, digital, and liquid-crystal thermometers simply from their own experiences of illness, but it is helpful for them to meet and discuss these different instruments in school as well.

Area: Area is usually the second 'derived' measure that children meet, after volume. The SI unit for area is the 'square metre' (m^2), derived from the base unit for length (m).

The intuitive idea underlying our conception of area is that of 'surface', and children need plenty of active experience with surfaces before attempting to measure them. Covering surfaces is helpful activity, so painting, tiling, jigsaw puzzles and so on are all beneficial early experiences.

Since area is measured with a derived unit there are strong connections between understanding multiplying as an arithmetic operation and work on measuring area; the two dimensions of any flat surface correspond helpfully to the two numbers involved in the binary operation of multiplying. Visual areas are a most effective illustration for many properties of multiplying, and multiplying is essential to the measuring of area.

Since there is such a close connection between multiplying and measuring area, formal work on measuring area is usually timed to coincide with a suitable stage in the development of children's calculating.

There are many interesting facets of our natural world to explore that relate surface areas with volumes and the significance of their relationships to biological life, e.g. babies and small creatures have *proportionally* much more surface area to their bodies in relation to their volume than adults and larger creatures. This is one key reason why babies and small creatures are much more vulnerable to extremes of heat and cold than adults and larger creatures, and also why small creatures have to eat so much more everyday (proportionally) than larger forms of life.

Measuring in Geometry, Measurement and Statistics 1

In these early activity groups attention is paid to discussing and discriminating between different lengths, capacities (and volumes), weights, and amounts of UK money; also to the succession and duration of events, and to telling the time.

This work in all areas is developed according to Stevens' classification of measuring scales in that the various attributes to be measured (length, capacity and so on) are firstly distinguished and named (*nominal*), then objects are compared according to those attributes and ordered (*ordinal*) before units (or regular *intervals*) are introduced. Finally, the standard *interval* scale for time is introduced.

Length and distance: Children are introduced to the wide variety of language used to refer to linear extension (e.g. 'length', 'width', 'height' and so on), and learn to compare and order lengths with each other, noting that comparisons depend upon both a common starting point and a 'straight' distance between two ends. Non-standard units are also introduced.

Weight: Children are introduced to the idea of weight as 'heaviness', and learn to compare and order the weights of objects using a pan balance. Non-standard units are introduced in order to describe the heaviness of a single object.

Capacity and volume: Children compare and order the capacities of a variety of containers, and are introduced to the idea of volume through capacity, that is, through the question, 'How much does this hold?' Non-standard units of capacity are introduced in the form of the capacities of relatively smaller vessels, e.g. the capacity of a large bottle measured by the number of yoghurt pots taken to fill it.

Time: Children are introduced to the ideas of duration in the form of days, weeks, hours, minutes and seconds and the succession of these units of time. They learn about our standard and everyday measures. Children also begin to learn

17 Technically, it is a measure of the thermal energy per particle of matter or radiation; it seems the 'hotter' something gets, the more those little things get agitated.

18 This means that as far as the Celsius scale is concerned, temperatures could go on getting ever hotter or colder 'forever'. Only the Kelvin scale acknowledges explicitly that in our universe it is presently thought impossible for temperatures to become any colder than $^{-}273{\cdot}15$°C.

to tell the time to the hour and half hour on an analogue clock. At this stage, succession is introduced through the regular cycles of everyday life, rather than use of a timeline.

Money: Children are introduced to the idea of economic 'worth' implicitly in the context of trade and markets, and quickly meet the idea of money as a collective measure of worth. Standard UK monies are introduced and relative values explored up to the value of £1. The *equivalence* of coins that so often puzzles children initially is explored thoroughly, and thus the equivalence of different amounts of cash.

Statistics during the primary years

As with measuring, no one ever uses statistics in real life without a specific *purpose* to it; in practice there is always some question or questions that people are trying to answer. Thus in work with children, any work on statistics should always be led by a key question (or questions) that shapes and directs the work itself.

The simplest of beginnings to statistics can be made with collections of real objects (perhaps things children bring back from a nature trail walk), about which a teacher could ask, 'So, what have we got here then?', and children can be encouraged to sift through, discriminate between and identify various categories into which objects can be sorted. Answers then become something like, 'We've got some of these, a few of those, only one of those' and so on. The objects themselves can then be displayed, grouped within their categories and suitably labelled.

Note how closely this activity relates to the use of 'nominal' scales in measuring; there is no ordering of objects or categories involved, simply a *discriminating between* objects. Such work is at the beginning of handling **categorical** data.

Thus sorting through a collection of real objects, noting similarities and differences and organizing the objects into categories in order to respond to a particular question, precedes similar activities with collections of data. The important thing is that the statistical activity is purposefully directed towards answering an initial specific question.

The data-handling cycle[19]

Purposeful statistics begins with a specific question (A) being posed. At the next stage (B) one identifies the kind(s) of data that would help answer the question. The following stage (C) is when the chosen data is collected, and then organized (including any visual representation) so as to reveal any patterns of significance relevant to answering the question posed. At stage (D) one interprets any patterns found at (C) in order to return and try to answer the question at (A).

It is always best to choose an initial question within an area of topical interest to the children. So for instance during some work on road safety children might be being advised to 'walk straight across' roads, rather than to cross them diagonally. Discussion could raise the point that it takes longer to cross a road diagonally than it does to go straight across, and therefore crossing diagonally puts a pedestrian in potential danger for longer. A relevant question (A) could be, 'How much more dangerous is it to cross a road diagonally, than it is to walk straight across?' Children could then (B) discuss what kinds of

19 See Graham, A. (1990) *Supporting Primary Mathematics: Handling Data*, Milton Keynes: The Open University, for a similar version.

data might help them to answer the question, and come up with the idea of marking out a 'road' on the playground and timing each child in the class both walking straight across and walking diagonally. Collecting and organizing the data so that comparisons can be made (perhaps involving the averaging of times) follows at stage (C), and then discussion (D) could interpret whether the time differences found at (C) help to answer question (A) well enough.

It may be that children feel the first run-through of the cycle answers the original question satisfactorily, in which case the work is over. Quite often however, a first run-through reveals that the initial question was not quite 'fit for purpose'; the question is then refined, and the whole cycle run through again on the basis of a different question at (A). It may be that in the road safety example, children decide it actually matters more *where* you cross a road, than whether you go exactly straight across – in which case a different question can be raised at point (A), perhaps timing how much warning you have of impending traffic if you try to cross a road near a bend.

Thus gradually one gets to understand the purpose of the statistical activity by increasing refinement of the task as repeated cycles are undertaken. Children get to appreciate how important it is to ask the right question in the first place, a range of data-collection techniques, data-organizing techniques, forms of pictorial and graphical representation, and approaches to interpretation, as different cycles are pursued.

In this important way, children come to realize that data handling and statistics are always undertaken for a specific purpose. That is, we do not construct graphs from data and then decide what questions those graphs could answer. We begin with a question, collect data, and then the construction a graph to show that data can help us to find the answer to the question.

Connections with measuring

Early measuring and early work on statistics are virtually indistinguishable from each other; in both types of activity children are learning to *distinguish between*, to *discriminate*, and to identify qualities that may be measured and related. Of course how various qualities may be related to each other will eventually take children to algebra and the study of relationships *in general*, and any calculating involved in statistics automatically relates back to their work in number. Everything is connected, in doing mathematics.

As children collect and analyse different kinds of data, in different kinds of ways, to answer a variety of questions, they will learn to *distinguish between* qualities, between *ordered* and un-ordered data, they will need *units* and utilize interval scales, and *compare* amounts multiplicatively using *ratio* scales. In all these ways the development of children's measuring is woven within the development of their work in statistics.

Statistics is a key context within which measuring demonstrates its own clear purposes.

There are no explicit statistics activities written for Geometry, Measurement and Statistics 1, although the sorting of shapes and of money that occur within geometry and measurement work respectively have clear relevance for the sorting of 'data' that will occur later.

Glossary

Most mathematical terms used in the *Geometry, Measurement and Statistics 1 Implementation Guide* and *Teaching Resource Handbook* can be found in a good mathematics dictionary such as the *Oxford Primary Illustrated Maths Dictionary*.

Other terms you might not be familiar with or which may provide particular challenges for children are explained in this glossary.

Bruner

Jerome Bruner (1915–) is a distinguished psychologist. His distinctions between enactive, iconic and symbolic representation have been particularly influential in the field of education.

communication mediator

A communication mediator is an object, image or action that helps communication in some way. These communication mediators need to be carefully introduced to children, for example Numicon Shapes and number rods become communication mediators when they help to illustrate discussions about the relationships between numbers, coins and lengths of time. However, there's no 'magic in the plastic' – a physical object or image is just a physical object or image unless it is actually supporting communication.

corner

Used in Geometry, Measurement and Statistics 1 to refer to the vertex of 2D and 3D shapes. The term 'vertex' is introduced in Geometry, Measurement and Statistics 2 to introduce the more formal geometrical name for a 'corner' or a point at which lines meet (see **edge**).

edge

Used to refer to a ridge on a 3D shape at which two faces or surfaces meet. Initially children may talk about both straight and curved edges; later, 'edge' refers only to boundaries of shapes which are straight lines. (See also **side**, **surface**.)

enactive, iconic and symbolic representation

Jerome Bruner (1966) distinguished three key ways in which we humans represent experience to ourselves: through enactive (internalized action), iconic (sensory) and symbolic (e.g. language-based) representations. In the Numicon approach we seek to combine all three forms of representation so that children experience number ideas through action, imagery and conversation.

flat shape

A two-dimensional (2D) shape, such as a rectangle, hexagon or oval. 'Flat' provides a physical and visual description which helps children distinguish or sort shapes of this type, and hence to develop mental imagery and generalize about them (see also **solid shape**).

generalization

A statement or observation (not necessarily correct) about a whole class of objects, situations or phenomena. Generalizations are essential and everywhere in mathematics – numbers, for example, are generalizations, as are shape names. For this reason children need to generalize and to work with generalizations constantly.

length

Length may refer to a dimension of an object, and in this sense be used to distinguish from width or breadth, height, thickness or distance. Alternatively, and perhaps confusingly for children, it can be used as a general term to describe all these measures of dimension.

mass

The amount of 'matter' in an object, which gives it heaviness or **weight** under gravity. The mass of an object is found by weighing it.

non-standard unit

In Geometry, Measurement and Statistics 1, children choose and use their own units to explore length, mass and capacity; they might measure a distance in steps, for example, or a capacity in scoops. These are non-standard units both in the sense that their size is not widely agreed (and may not even be fixed), and in the sense that they are not commonly used for making exact measurements. Rather they are practical, everyday-world measures which enable children to access and investigate ideas of measurement as they work towards understanding and using 'standard' units such as metres, kilograms or litres.

number fact

The term 'number fact' usually refers to an operation on two or more numbers, together with its outcome. So '6 + 3 = 9' is a number 'fact', as is '256 ÷ 16 = 16'. In UK schools simple addition and subtraction facts are often referred to as 'number bonds'.

number names/objects/words

Adults often use number words such as 'four' or 'twenty-three' as nouns, and ask children questions such as 'What is seven and three?' In our language, nouns name objects, so we commonly (and unconsciously) assume that number words must be being used to name number objects – thus numbers are often treated as if they are objects.

It is important to remember that we don't always use number words as nouns; quite often we use those same words as adjectives, as in 'Can you get me three spoons?' One of the key puzzles for children to solve is when to use number words as adjectives, and when as nouns.

number sentence

The metaphor of a 'sentence' – in the sense of a unit of language – is sometimes used to describe a number fact written horizontally, left to right, as in '4 + 23 = 27'.

numerals

Numerals function as shorthand for number words. The numeral '5' is shorthand for the word 'five'. When used as a noun, the numeral '5' is often said to represent or stand for the number object we call 'five'.

Numicon Shape pattern

The system of arranging objects or images (up to ten in number) in pairs alongside each other; this is also sometimes called 'the pair-wise tens frame'. Fig. 1 shows the Numicon 7-pattern.

Numicon Shape

Numicon Shapes are pieces of coloured plastic with from one to ten holes, arranged in the pattern of a pair-wise tens frame (see Fig. 2).

oblong

A **rectangle** which is not a square – that is, a 2D shape with four straight sides and four right angles in which one pair of sides are longer that the other pair (see Fig. 3).

parts and properties

The **properties** of a shape are defined by how its **parts**, e.g. 'vertices' and 'edges', relate to each other. For example, one property of a trapezium is that it has just two sides that are parallel to each other. A property of a rectangle is adjacent sides meeting at 90°.

Piaget

Jean Piaget (1896–1980) was a philosopher and psychologist who spent years studying young children and how they learn. He believed that the development of knowledge is based on developing cognitive structures and that children should be actively involved in their own learning.

rectangle

A 2D shape with four straight sides and four right angles. This means that a square is also a rectangle – a special case in which the four sides are also of equal length – and all other rectangles are **oblongs** (see Fig. 3).

side

Used to refer to a boundary or edge of a 2D shape which joins two corners. Initially children may talk about both straight and curved sides; later, 'side' refers only to boundaries of shapes which are straight lines. (See also **corner**, **edge**.)

solid shape

A three-dimensional (3D) shape, such as a cube, sphere or cone. 'Solid' provides a physical and visual description which helps children distinguish or sort shapes of this type, and hence to develop mental imagery and generalize about them (see also **flat shape**).

surface

Used in Geometry, Measurement and Statistics 1 to refer to the surface of a 3D shape; it may be flat, as in a cube, or curved, as in a sphere. The term 'face', which describes a flat surface only, is introduced in Geometry, Measurement and Statistics 2.

weight

The heaviness of an object. By weighing an object to find out how heavy it is, we also find out how much 'matter' it contains – that is, what its **mass** is. The standard unit used to measure weight is Newtons; the standard units for measuring mass are kilograms and grams.

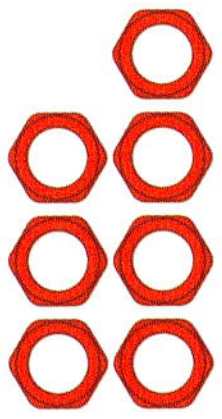

1

2

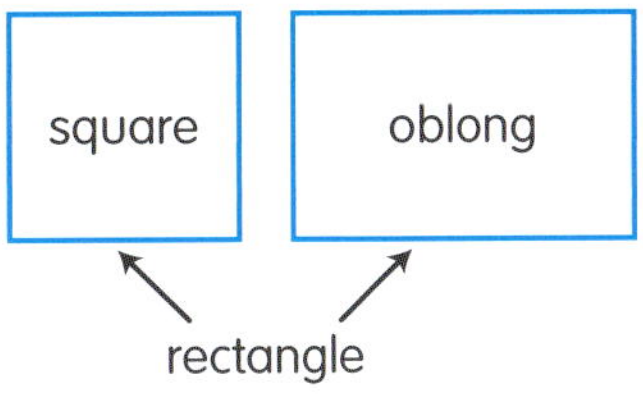

3